MASS GATHERING SECURITY: A LOOK AT THE COORDINATED APPROACH TO SUPER BOWL XLVIII IN NEW JERSEY AND OTHER LARGE-SCALE EVENTS

FIELD HEARING

BEFORE THE

SUBCOMMITTEE ON EMERGENCY PREPAREDNESS, RESPONSE, AND COMMUNICATIONS

OF THE

COMMITTEE ON HOMELAND SECURITY HOUSE OF REPRESENTATIVES

ONE HUNDRED THIRTEENTH CONGRESS

SECOND SESSION

JUNE 23, 2014

Serial No. 113–73

Printed for the use of the Committee on Homeland Security

Available via the World Wide Web: http://www.gpo.gov/fdsys/

U.S. GOVERNMENT PRINTING OFFICE

90–883 PDF WASHINGTON : 2014

For sale by the Superintendent of Documents, U.S. Government Printing Office
Internet: bookstore.gpo.gov Phone: toll free (866) 512–1800; DC area (202) 512–1800
Fax: (202) 512–2250 Mail: Stop SSOP, Washington, DC 20402–0001

COMMITTEE ON HOMELAND SECURITY

MICHAEL T. MCCAUL, Texas, *Chairman*

LAMAR SMITH, Texas
PETER T. KING, New York
MIKE ROGERS, Alabama
PAUL C. BROUN, Georgia
CANDICE S. MILLER, Michigan, *Vice Chair*
PATRICK MEEHAN, Pennsylvania
JEFF DUNCAN, South Carolina
TOM MARINO, Pennsylvania
JASON CHAFFETZ, Utah
STEVEN M. PALAZZO, Mississippi
LOU BARLETTA, Pennsylvania
RICHARD HUDSON, North Carolina
STEVE DAINES, Montana
SUSAN W. BROOKS, Indiana
SCOTT PERRY, Pennsylvania
MARK SANFORD, South Carolina
VACANCY

BENNIE G. THOMPSON, Mississippi
LORETTA SANCHEZ, California
SHEILA JACKSON LEE, Texas
YVETTE D. CLARKE, New York
BRIAN HIGGINS, New York
CEDRIC L. RICHMOND, Louisiana
WILLIAM R. KEATING, Massachusetts
RON BARBER, Arizona
DONALD M. PAYNE, JR., New Jersey
BETO O'ROURKE, Texas
FILEMON VELA, Texas
ERIC SWALWELL, California
VACANCY
VACANCY

BRENDAN P. SHIELDS, *Staff Director*
MICHAEL GEFFROY, *Deputy Staff Director/Chief Counsel*
MICHAEL S. TWINCHEK, *Chief Clerk*
I. LANIER AVANT, *Minority Staff Director*

SUBCOMMITTEE ON EMERGENCY PREPAREDNESS, RESPONSE, AND COMMUNICATIONS

SUSAN W. BROOKS, Indiana, *Chairwoman*

PETER T. KING, New York
STEVEN M. PALAZZO, Mississippi, *Vice Chair*
SCOTT PERRY, Pennsylvania
MARK SANFORD, South Carolina
MICHAEL T. MCCAUL, Texas *(ex officio)*

DONALD M. PAYNE, JR., New Jersey
YVETTE D. CLARKE, New York
BRIAN HIGGINS, New York
BENNIE G. THOMPSON, Mississippi *(ex officio)*

ERIC B. HEIGHBERGER, *Subcommittee Staff Director*
DEBORAH JORDAN, *Subcommittee Clerk*

CONTENTS

MASS GATHERING SECURITY: A LOOK AT THE COORDINATED APPROACH TO SUPER BOWL XLVIII IN NEW JERSEY AND OTHER LARGE-SCALE EVENTS

Monday, June 23, 2014

U.S. House of Representatives,
Subcommittee on Emergency Preparedness,
Response, and Communications,
Committee on Homeland Security,
University Heights, NJ.

The subcommittee met, pursuant to call, at 10:00 a.m., at New Jersey Institute of Technology Auditorium, University Heights, Hon. Susan W. Brooks [Chairwoman of the subcommittee] presiding.

Present: Representatives Brooks and Payne.

Also present: Representative Pascrell.

Mrs. BROOKS. The Committee on Homeland Security Subcommittee on Emergency Preparedness, Response, and Communications will now come to order.

The subcommittee is meeting today to examine mass gathering security.

First I would like to thank everybody, particularly Dr. Bloom and his staff and everyone at NJIT, for working with our staff in setting up this outstanding field hearing location. I know it takes a lot of work and effort, and it is wonderful to be on your campus. Prior to coming to Congress, I also was in higher education, and it is just wonderful to see such a distinguished campus and a distinguished university and to learn about your fine university.

I also want to thank my Ranking Member, Congressman Payne, for suggesting after the Super Bowl that was hosted here that we convene this hearing, and it was wonderful to be in your home town. Arrived last evening, saw a beautiful military park and watched U.S. tie Portugal, and had a lovely evening last night, with the exception of that tie at the very end. But I do appreciate everyone for coming today and participating in this important field hearing, as well as Congressman Pascrell. We are so pleased, representing New Jersey's 9th District, for you taking your time away from your district to be a part of this.

He has been a leader in homeland security and issues involving our National security, so we are very pleased to have you here today.

This is an official Congressional hearing as opposed to a town hall meeting, and so there are some House rules. We need to make

(1)

sure that our audience—and we are so pleased today to have so many people participate—that we abide by certain rules of the Committee on Homeland Security and of the House. I kindly wish to remind our guests today that demonstrations from the audience, which include even applause or any verbal outbursts, as well as any signs or placards, are a violation of rules of the House. So you may really like what you hear, but this is a formal hearing, much like in a courtroom. So it is important that we respect the decorum and the rules of the House.

So now I will recognize myself for an opening statement.

As the world looks on, millions gather in Brazil to watch the World Cup, and the subcommittee is meeting today, I think in a very timely way, to examine the security considerations necessary for mass gatherings.

On February 2, 2014, Super Bowl XLVIII took place less than 10 miles from where we are sitting today. That event, which was attended by more than 80,000 people and watched around the world by more than 100 million people, is just one of the many large sporting events and gatherings that take place around the country each and every year.

My home State of Indiana, and Indianapolis in particular, are very accustomed to hosting large events as well. Year after year, we welcome hundreds of thousands of visitors who attend conventions, sporting events, festivals, and other mass gatherings. Events such as the Indianapolis 500, Big 10 Championship games, all with hundreds of thousands of attendees and athletes, occur annually. Additionally, my home city of Indianapolis has hosted multiple NCAA Final Four Championships, and in 2012 we were the proud sponsors and proud to host Super Bowl XLVI.

During the events leading up to Super Bowl XLVI, Indianapolis catered to nearly 1.1 million visitors in Super Bowl Village. We also host the largest capacity sports venue in the world, the Indianapolis Motor Speedway. This venue has a seating capacity—and think about this—of more than 250,000 spectators at any one time. It is the largest single event, spectator event in the country, and it is held every Memorial Day weekend, and we regularly have race day attendance of over 300,000 spectators.

But to be successful, all of these events, including Super Bowl XLVI, each of these events take years of planning and coordination between officials at all levels of government with their private-sector partners. Because of the nature of these events, we know that a significant amount of time and money must be spent on security and planning for every eventuality.

Unfortunately, in 2011, in my home State of Indiana, we experienced a tragedy at the 2011 Indiana State Fair, where a microburst, or like a mini-tornado, caused a stage to collapse at a significant large concert, resulting in the tragic loss of 7 lives and required an incredible significant emergency response. Sadly, twice over the last year we were again reminded of what is at stake at events of this magnitude. On Monday, April 15, 2013, at roughly 2:50 in the afternoon, two explosive devices detonated near the finish line of the Boston Marathon. The terrorist attack there resulted in 3 deaths and approximately 260 injuries. The IEDs used in this attack were made from pressure cookers, toy car parts, and gunpowder taken from fireworks. Although a tragic event, the response in the aftermath of that bombing proved that the coordination and planning that took place prior to that event was a huge success.

Additionally, just a few days before the Super Bowl here, a suspicious powder was mailed to several locations in New Jersey and New York, including hotels near the Super Bowl site. Thankfully, those substances were non-toxic, but the situation served as a stark reminder of the threats we face and the importance of planning, training, and exercises prior to these mass gatherings.

One of the keys to success is thorough planning and coordination. That includes at all levels—Federal, State, local, and private sector. It involves intelligence personnel, first responders, security experts, and dozens of other players who have a part to play.

In preparation for Super Bowl XLVIII, the Department of Homeland Security took the lead in coordinating Federal efforts to assist the New Jersey State Police in security operations at MetLife Stadium and the surrounding areas, directing over 13 Federal offices and agencies in a massive interagency partnership. This partnership included the FBI, Department of Health and Human Services, FDA, and DOD, among others, all essential partners.

I am pleased today that we are joined by key stakeholders and the key leaders who planned those efforts. Each of our witnesses played a vital role in ensuring the safety and security of the public when they attend mass gatherings. I look forward to hearing their perspectives on their successes and challenges in planning not only for the Super Bowl but also for the Indianapolis 500, and the best practices that you have used and how we share those.

At this time, I would like to yield to the distinguished gentleman from New Jersey, Ranking Member of the subcommittee, Mr. Payne, for his opening statement.

Mr. PAYNE. Thank you, Madam Chairwoman.

It is a real honor and a privilege to be able to host this site visit and have such a distinguished panel before us, and the second one as well, to discuss these important issues on mass gatherings.

So I am happy that the Subcommittee on Emergency Preparedness, Response, and Communications has the opportunity to come to the 10th Congressional District of New Jersey to learn about the unique challenges the State faced in preparing for the Super Bowl. I think this is a good opportunity to also learn about how the Federal, State, and local governments and the private sector work together to address the challenges in preparing for a major National event.

Before I begin, I would once again like to thank Chairwoman Brooks for holding today's hearing here in New Jersey and invite a good friend and a gentleman that was part of the original Homeland Security Committee and has passed the baton on to me in good stead. The homeland is in good shape, but we have to continue to be vigilant. But I would like to thank Mr. Pascrell for taking the time to be here and being such a mentor for me since I have arrived in Congress.

States and cities across the United States can learn much from the unprecedented preparedness efforts carried out by first responders from Newark to Jersey City to Rutherford and across the State.

I would like to thank Eric Heiberger, Kerry Kinirons, and Kate Bonnevecchio from the Majority staff; Tiffany Hoss, Maura Bergen, and Ashely Delgado from the Minority staff; and Natalie Nixon and Debbie Jordan, committee clerks, for making today's panel possible.

Finally, I would like to thank the New Jersey Institute of Technology for hosting this hearing in such a beautiful space. NJIT is the home of the Homeland Security Technology System Center and the Homeland Security and Emergency Management Program. To Mr. Bloom, we couldn't have picked a more wonderful site. I feel at home. I have spent a lot of time in this room, so the familiarity helps to have a conducive environment to hold this.

These impressive programs make important contributions to our ability to identify and address vulnerabilities to National and State security and the development of well-trained, highly-skilled emergency management personnel. Before 9/11, the focus of security professionals at our Nation's sporting arenas and other venues for mass gatherings focused primarily on crowd containment and firearm entry prevention. After 9/11, these spaces with significant crowd capacity and media presence became prime targets for terrorist activity. Preventing, preparing for, and responding to a terrorist attack or other disaster at a sporting event requires close coordination between Federal, State, and local authorities.

Venue owners, sporting associations, and event promoters have worked together with Federal, State, and local law enforcement and emergency managers to develop, implement, and exercise plans to counter the evolving threats posed.

The National Football League has the highest game attendance of any domestic professional sports league in the world, drawing over 68,400 spectators per game for its most recently completed season in 2013. Its largest widely-attended event is the Super Bowl, which had an attendance of more than 82,000 spectators at MetLife Stadium on February 2, 2014. It is a testament to the coordinated efforts that such a massive event occurred without incident.

The success of the February 2, 2014 Super Bowl is a credit to over a decade's worth of building preparedness and response capabilities at the local and State level with Homeland Security grant investments, and in a year-and-a-half of coordination, planning exercises, Federal, State, and local law enforcement and first responders, alongside the private sector.

In November 2013, I led a New Jersey delegation briefing to learn about the Federal security preparations. Two months later, I participated in a site visit at MetLife Stadium, at which time Lieutenant Colonel Cetnar described that State Police coordinated security efforts with entities ranging from the Federal Government to the Port Authority of New York and New Jersey to local governments throughout the region. At each of the briefings, I was impressed by the degree of planning and coordination across all levels of the government and jurisdictions.

By the time the Super Bowl arrived, I was very confident in the preparations that had taken place, and I commend the Federal, the State, and the local enforcement on their success.

I would also like to congratulate the NFL and MetLife Stadium on their work to enhance security efforts prior to the Super Bowl.

I am pleased that in addition to learning about advances in the mass gathering security here in New Jersey, we will have an opportunity to learn about the security efforts at the Indianapolis Motor Speedway. These opportunities to share best practices and lessons learned are invaluable.

Finally, as we look to the future of mass gathering security, I would be interested to learn from the witnesses, particularly Dr. Roberts, about the type of threats we will face in the future and how the Federal Government can help address them.

Again, I thank Chairwoman Brooks for holding this hearing, and Congressman Pascrell for participating. I appreciate her partnership and willingness to work together with me on important homeland security priorities, including mass gatherings security. I look forward to the testimony from our talented panels, and I yield back the balance of my time.

Mrs. BROOKS. At this time, the Chairwoman now recognizes Congressman Pascrell from New Jersey's 9th District for a few opening remarks.

Mr. PASCRELL. Chairwoman Brooks, thank you for inviting me. I really appreciate that; and, of course, my buddy here, Donald Payne. It is good to be back on the homeland. It was a bipartisan effort that started us after 9/11, and with the deepest respect for the oath that we take, that is the first thing that we pledge, to support and defend the Nation from outside as well as inside. So we are talking about terrorists from outside and inside this Nation.

Dr. Bloom, this great institution, we worked together on many projects, including the Smart Gun, and thank you for never being afraid of reasonable gun violence legislation. I really do salute you for that.

As co-chairman of Public Safety Advisory Committee in the Congress, this is in my bone marrow. Preparing and coordinating capabilities whenever there is a mass gathering, a large gathering, is an awesome task, and we really need to salute law enforcement on all levels who understand coordination. On 9/11, we had very little coordination. I mean, we mouthed coordination, but it did not exist. One of the reasons for the devastation on 9/11 is because one group didn't speak to another group.

That has changed—not 100 percent, but it has changed for the better. So al-Qaeda's manual for jihad proposed football stadiums in that manual as a possible terrorist attack site, and the FBI issued an alert in 2002 warning that people with links to terrorist groups were downloading those stadium images. Thanks to the FBI for a lot that has advanced over the past 13 years.

Now, the Supporting Anti-Terrorism by Fostering Effective Technologies, the SAFETY Act, was enacted in the Homeland Security Act of 2002. The goal of promoting development of anti-terrorism technologies by providing civil liability protections when certified technologies are deployed to protect against terrorism are defeated by an act of terrorism.

So this is an awesome task. I want to thank the committee. As Bill Bradley used to say, another Jersey guy, Bill Bradley would always watch the person without the ball. That is what made him a great basketball player. He understood his role.

I followed your career, Congresswoman Brooks. You come from a great part of the country, and you are doing a great job, and I am here to do whatever I can to help you and Don Payne do their jobs. God bless you, and thank you for coming to Jersey.

Mrs. BROOKS. Thank you very much. I must say that I have very much appreciated the bipartisan nature in which Homeland Security as a committee of the whole and our subcommittee in particular have worked together.

Mr. PASCRELL. That is right, very rare.

Mrs. BROOKS. We pledge to continue to do that. It is so important. Citizens expect it, and particularly our law enforcement and first responders expect it. So thank you for your leadership.

We are pleased to have two panels of very distinguished witnesses before us today on this important topic. Our first panel is before us, and Congressman Payne will now introduce and give brief introductions of our first panel.

Mr. PAYNE. Thank you, Madam Chairwoman.

With us today we have Andrew McLees, and he serves as special agent in charge for immigration and customs enforcement in Newark's field office, a position he has held since August 2011. In November 2012, he was appointed by the Secretary of Homeland Security to serve as the Federal coordinator for Super Bowl XLVIII. Special Agent McLees has held a number of positions with ICE, including chief of staff at ICE headquarters and as the deputy special agent in charge in Philadelphia's office. He began his law enforcement career in 1989 with the United States Customs Service.

Welcome, sir.

Edward Cetnar serves as the deputy superintendent of the New Jersey State Police and was appointed as the incident commander and principal security planner for Super Bowl XLVIII. Lieutenant Colonel Cetnar joined the New Jersey State Police in 1987. He also is an adjunct professor at Seton Hall University, teaching courses in Human Resources and Education.

Welcome. Go Hall.

Louis Koumoutsos serves as chief of the Port Authority Police Department, a position to which he was appointed in May 2013. He is a 21-year veteran of the Department and was instrumental in the response to and recovery from both the September 11 attacks on the World Trade Center and Hurricane Sandy.

Welcome, sir.

Chief John Centanni is the fire chief for the city of Newark, a position he has held since 2010. He has previously served as the chief of staff to the fire director. Chief Centanni joined the Newark Fire Department in 1986.

Welcome.

Mrs. BROOKS. I want to thank our witnesses for also providing full written statements, and they will appear in the record, so I want to thank you for your time with respect to those statements.

I just want to let you know, and for those in the audience just a reminder, that the green, yellow, and red light—it turns green during your testimony, it will become yellow when you have a minute left to speak, and red. If you could just wrap up your comments shortly after the red light goes off. Also, this mic system, you need to push it in order to speak and to push the button again when you are finished speaking. So I just want to remind you of those.

The Chairwoman now will recognize Special Agent McLees for 5 minutes of testimony.

STATEMENT OF ANDREW MCLEES, SPECIAL AGENT IN CHARGE, FEDERAL COORDINATING OFFICER, IMMIGRATION AND CUSTOMS ENFORCEMENT, U.S. DEPARTMENT OF HOMELAND SECURITY

Mr. MCLEES. Chairwoman Brooks, Ranking Member Payne, and Congressman Pascrell, thank you for the opportunity to appear before you today to discuss DHS' role in supporting comprehensive efforts to safely secure mass gatherings and large-scale public events in the United States.

Specifically, I would like to discuss my role as the Federal coordinator assigned to be the primary Federal point of contact for facilitating planning efforts in support of the New Jersey State Police for Super Bowl XLVIII.

In November 2012, then-Secretary Napolitano appointed me to serve as the Federal coordinator for the Super Bowl XLVIII, and over the course of the following 18 months DHS played an instrumental role in preparing for and supporting the security efforts for the Super Bowl. As part of the special security events annual planning process, DHS requested that all State and local governments submit information related to any special events taking place within their jurisdiction. Using an algorithm that incorporates information provided by these jurisdictions such as attendance, facility type, and iconic value, among other measures, the event is designated on a scale known as a Special Event Assessment Rating, or SEAR, 1 through 5.

The Super Bowl is annually a SEAR 1. Another recent example of a SEAR designation was the Indianapolis 500, which was designated as a SEAR 2. This designation is what triggers the appointment of the Federal Coordination Team which is drawn from the local jurisdiction of the event to capitalize on the existing relationships in that community.

The Federal Coordination Team was responsible for coordinating and the integrated planning for and use of Federal resources from over 30 agencies across the spectrum of prevention, protection, response, and recovery. Members of the team were pre-staged to perform their roles as advisors to the local incident command at key command and control centers prior to and during the event, including the State Police's Public Safety Compound, the FBI Intelligence Operations Center, as well as MetLife Stadium.

The Federal Coordination Team was directly supported by DHS Operations and Special Events Program based in Washington. This group is responsible for the risk assessment process, the Federal interagency information sharing, and support resourcing for special events. They also provide the conduit to the Secretary of DHS and the Federal interagency.

The needs of the State Police in addressing this mass gathering were identified in one of two ways. One method was in walking the ground and working alongside the State Police. This enabled the Federal Coordination Team to better understand and identify vulnerabilities facing the event and make known the spectrum of Federal resources available. The other method was derived during the pre-incident planning process and resulted in direct requests from the State Police.

One example of a direct request I received from the State Police was to facilitate the establishment of a temporary flight restriction zone near MetLife Stadium on Super Bowl Sunday. I was able to accomplish this by coordinating with the FAA, who controls the air space; the Department of Defense, who are responsible for air defense; and Customs and Border Protection's Air and Marine Operations, who provided the assets to conduct low and slow air intercept operations.

In addition to CBP's efforts, the TSA provided assets to ensure the overall safety of fans by staffing the event from a rail transit perspective, as well as assigning additional personnel to assist with the mass overflow of travelers the day after the game through local airports. The Secret Service leant their cyber expertise in an area that is critical and continues to evolve, and these are just a few examples of how DHS components work closely with and in support of the State Police to secure the event and related venues.

In addition to our support for security operations, we also played a significant role in preserving and protecting commercial aspects of the Super Bowl. ICE's efforts were primarily related to counterfeit NFL merchandising game tickets. In September 2013, ICE initiated Operation Team Player, a multi-agency initiative designed to combat intellectual property rights violations. As a result of our National enforcement operations, we seized over 350,000 items valued at $37 million.

Both DHS and ICE remain committed to supporting our Federal, State, local, and private-sector partners to ensure that all future mass gatherings and large-scale public events held in the United States are safe. It is our mission to provide security, consequence management, and law enforcement resources so that these events are incident-free and successful. We will build upon the success of our involvement with providing resources and support for the prior Super Bowls, the recent Indianapolis 500, and other previously-held events, and will continue to impart our lessons learned for the safety and security of all future mass gatherings.

Finally, I would like to recognize and publicly thank the New Jersey State Police Incident Command, Major Kevin Fowler, Major Bob Yaiser, and, of course, Lieutenant Colonel Cetnar. I was proud to work alongside these dedicated professionals who provided superior leadership, expertise, and camaraderie that resulted in a well-organized and incident-free Super Bowl.

Thank you again for inviting me to appear before you today and for your continued support of DHS, ICE, and all the agencies that contributed to protecting the Super Bowl. I would be pleased to answer any questions. Thank you.

[The prepared statement of Mr. McLees follows:]

PREPARED STATEMENT OF ANDREW MCLEES

JUNE 23, 2014

INTRODUCTION

Chairwoman Brooks, Ranking Member Payne, and distinguished Members of the subcommittee: As the special agent in charge for Homeland Security Investigations (HSI), U.S. Immigration and Customs Enforcement (ICE) in Newark, I would like to thank you for inviting me to share with you information about the role of the Department of Homeland Security (DHS) in supporting the comprehensive efforts to safely secure mass gatherings and large-scale public events in the United States. Specifically, I would like to discuss my role as the Federal coordinator assigned to be the primary Federal point of contact for facilitating coordinated Federal planning efforts for Super Bowl XLVIII.

As part of this important effort, I was honored to work alongside the gentlemen sitting with me today, Lt. Colonial Ed Cetnar of the New Jersey State Police (NJSP) and Chief Louis Koumoutsos of the Port Authority Police Department, in our collective mission to ensure that the Super Bowl was free from any significant security incident before, during, and after the game.

DHS'S ROLE IN SECURITY EFFORTS FOR SUPER BOWL XLVIII

In November 2012, then-Secretary Napolitano appointed me to serve as the Federal coordinator for Super Bowl XVLIII, which was played on February 2, 2014, at MetLife Stadium in New Jersey. Over the course of the following 18 months, DHS played an instrumental role in preparing for and supporting the security efforts for the Super Bowl. As the Federal coordinator, I worked in partnership with two Deputy Federal coordinators: James Mottola, special agent in charge for the U.S. Secret Service (USSS) in Newark, and Frank Westfall, regional director for the Office of Infrastructure Protection within DHS's National Protection and Programs Directorate (NPPD). I served as the Secretary's representative and primary Federal point of contact for facilitating coordinated Federal planning in support of the event's incident command and the New Jersey State Police (NJSP).

As part of the Special Security Events yearly planning process, DHS requests that all State and local governments submit information related to any special events taking place within their jurisdiction for the following year. Using an algorithm that incorporates information provided by the State and local jurisdictions, such as attendance, facility type, and iconic value among other measures, the event is designated on a scale known as the Special Event Assessment Rating (SEAR) 1 through 5. A National Special Security Event (NSSE) is not evaluated and designated in the same manner. NSSEs are assessed based upon a separate data submission provided by the lead State and/or local agency on behalf of the Governor of the State in which the event is held. The Super Bowl is annually designated as a SEAR 1, which is the highest rating other than that of an NSSE.

The Super Bowl XVLIII Federal Coordination Team was responsible for coordinating the integrated planning for and use of Federal resources from over 30 Federal agencies across the spectrum of prevention, protection, response, and recovery. Members of the Federal Coordination Team were pre-staged to perform their role as advisors to local incident command at key command and control centers prior to and during the event, including the NJSP Public Safety Compound, the NJSP Venue Incident Command Post, the Federal Bureau of Investigation (FBI) Intelligence Operations Center (IOC), as well as the stadium. In the event of an incident, my role as the Federal coordinator would have been to serve in an advisory capacity to the NJSP.

The Federal Coordination Team was directly supported by the DHS Office of Operations Coordination and Planning, Special Events Program, based in Washington, DC. This group is responsible for the risk assessment process, Federal interagency information sharing, and support resourcing for special events. In addition, they also provide the structure and subject-matter expertise to assure Federal coordinator consistency and provide the conduit to the Secretary, DHS, and the Federal interagency.

FEDERAL COORDINATION AND OPERATIONAL EFFORTS SUPPORTING THE EVENT

Federal Coordination Team.—During the planning process, the Federal Coordination Team was embedded with the NJSP and acted in consultation with the NJSP Incident Command. It was our responsibility to ensure that the appropriate Federal support was provided in response to requests for assistance from Federal, State, and local partners. It is important to underscore the mechanisms by which the Federal

Coordination Team coordinated the use of DHS and other Federal assets because it highlights the best practice of a diverse team with strong, local relationships. The responsiveness of DHS and the team was an important message we wanted our security partners to have throughout the process.

The needs of the NJSP in addressing this mass gathering were identified in one of two ways. One method was in "walking the ground" and working alongside our NJSP partners. This enabled the Federal Coordination Team to better understand and identify the vulnerabilities facing the event, and make known the spectrum of Federal resources available. The other method was derived during the pre-incident planning process and resulted in direct NJSP requests for assistance to the Federal coordinator.

One example of a direct request that I received from the NJSP was to facilitate the establishment of a temporary flight restriction zone in the vicinity of MetLife Stadium on Super Bowl Sunday. I was able to accomplish this by coordinating with the Federal Aviation Administration (FAA), which controls the airspace; the Department of Defense, which is responsible for air defense; and U.S. Customs and Border Protection (CBP) Air and Marine Operations, which provided assets to conduct low and slow air intercept operations, and patrol the critical rail link between Secaucus Junction and MetLife Stadium in support of New Jersey Transit.

CBP.—CBP supplied aircraft equipped with video downlink feeds of the venues to the Public Safety Compound, the Regional Operations Intelligence Center, and the Intelligence Operations Center, all coordinated with the NJSP Aviation Unit. This allowed public safety officials appropriate situational awareness in order to address crowd control, traffic, and other incidents. Diversion airports were identified outside the restricted zone to divert violators of the flight restriction where they would be met by FBI Special Agents and Transportation Security Administration (TSA) Federal Air Marshals. At the request of the NJSP, I coordinated with CBP's Office of Field Operations to initiate Vehicle and Cargo Inspection System (VACIS) operations to screen cargo and vehicles destined for secure Super Bowl venues through non-intrusive inspection technology. In addition, CBP provided support to FBI tactical teams.

USCG.—Existing professional relationships and knowledge of available resources allowed for coordination informally. For instance, there was a request to establish a maritime security environment to secure the waterways adjacent to various Super Bowl venues. This was accomplished between the NJSP Marine Unit and the U.S. Coast Guard, which already work side-by-side on a daily basis year-round.

TSA.—The Transportation Security Administration (TSA) provided assets to ensure the overall efficiency and safety of fans by staffing the event from a rail transit perspective, as well as assigning additional personnel to assist with the mass outflow of travelers the day after the game through local airports. TSA's Federal Air Marshals assisted in securing the event by assigning marshals to ride the mass transit system, performing the same role as they do in the aviation environment. TSA also assigned Visible Intermodal Prevention and Response (VIPR) teams in critical transfer and origination rail stations.

ICE.—The Federal Government assisted in addressing criminal enterprises related to the Super Bowl. There were three key areas that Federal law enforcement committed significant resources: Addressing the threat to cybersecurity; investigating human trafficking; and the protection of intellectual property.

While my agency worked with the FBI on combating human trafficking surrounding the event, our efforts in the criminal enterprise realm were primarily related to counterfeit National Football League (NFL) merchandise and counterfeit game tickets. In September 2013, ICE initiated Operation Team Player, a multiagency initiative in conjunction with other law enforcement agencies and the NFL. This operation was designed to combat intellectual property rights violations that are typically associated with large-scale sporting events. In July 2013, for example, HSI Newark worked in coordination with the ICE-led Intellectual Property Rights Center, the NFL and other professional and collegiate sports leagues to host training for over 200 Federal, State, and local officers who also enforce intellectual property violations.

During the operational period leading up to the game, HSI Newark led daily enforcement operations targeting the sale of counterfeit NFL apparel, merchandise, and Super Bowl tickets. National enforcement operations resulted in the seizure of over 350,000 items with an estimated retail value of $37 million and 76 arrests. HSI special agents also investigated the sale of counterfeit Super Bowl tickets, and seized 163 counterfeit tickets valued at approximately $170,000.

USSS.—In addition to the appointment of Special Agent in Charge Mottola as the deputy Federal coordinator for this event, the USSS assigned other personnel to provide training and conduct threat assessments for all critical infrastructure components connected to the event, including MetLife Stadium. They also were assigned to Cyber Response Teams before and during the event with the capability to address a cyber-related attack on any entity connected to the Super Bowl.

The USSS assigned personnel from the Protective Intelligence and Assessment Division who reviewed open-source information that provided real-time awareness on public safety matters that could have adversely impacted the game. The USSS Uniformed Division officers provided magnetometer training to the private security services manning the check points at MetLife Stadium. Additionally, the USSS was responsible for coordinating the protective advance for former President Clinton, who attended the game.

FEMA.—The Federal Emergency Management Agency (FEMA) was another key partner. FEMA personnel were on-site, prepared to coordinate Federal resources, in support of State and local response efforts in mitigating the consequences of a natural disaster or terrorist attack. As part of its responsibilities, FEMA personnel led the planning for such a contingency.

DHS Headquarters.—At the DHS Headquarters level, NPPD supported the effort of minimizing risk to critical infrastructure through identification, assessment, and monitoring of threats and vulnerabilities in the designated geographical areas of responsibility in support of the Super Bowl.

Deputy Federal Coordinator Westfall was the lead field representative for NPPD's Office of Infrastructure Protection supporting the security planning and other preparedness efforts. He facilitated or completed 25 facility security surveys, vulnerability assessments, Computer-Based Assessment Tools and Cyber Security Resilience Reviews on key event venues and supporting infrastructure, including MetLife Stadium, the MetLife Sports Complex, and the Public Service Electric & Gas Company (PSE&G) East Rutherford Switching Station.

The DHS Office of Intelligence and Analysis (I&A) deployed intelligence personnel who provided analytic support, facilitated information exchange, and assisted event leadership in developing and prioritizing protective and support measures for Super Bowl pre-event and event intelligence, information sharing, and planning. In addition, I&A conducted Classified and Unclassified cyber engagements in November 2013 with the U.S. Attorney for the District of New Jersey, the Federal Coordination Team for the Super Bowl, the NJSP Incident Command, and the New Jersey Cyber Cell, including the New Jersey Homeland Security Advisor, Fusion Center Director, and private-sector partners. These engagements enabled Federal, State, local, and private-sector stakeholders to improve cybersecurity and increase cyber resilience prior to the event. I&A also maintained a secure communication facility at the Public Safety Compound during game. Other DHS Headquarters elements, including the Office of Science and Technology, the Office of Domestic Nuclear Detection, and the Office of Health Affairs provided technical support to the event.

Federal Partners.—Outside of DHS, the FBI, the U.S. Marshals Service, the U.S. Department of Energy National Nuclear Security Administration, the U.S. Department of Health and Human Services, and the U.S. Department of Commerce's National Weather Service all provided additional support and specific expertise to our efforts.

CONCLUSION

ICE and the other operating components and Headquarters elements of DHS are committed to supporting our Federal, State, local, and private-sector partners to ensure the safety and security of future mass gatherings and large-scale public events held in the United States. We will work together to provide security, consequence management, and law enforcement resources so that these events are incident-free and successful. We will build upon the success of our involvement in providing resources in support of prior Super Bowls, the recent Indianapolis 500 race, and other previously-held events, and will continue to impart our lessons learned for the safety and security of all future mass gatherings.

In addition to Colonel Fuentes of the NJSP and FBI Special Agent in Charge Ford here in Newark, I would also like to recognize and thank the NJSP Incident Command, Lt. Colonial Ed Cetnar, as well as Major Kevin Fowler and Major Bob Yaiser. I was proud to work alongside these dedicated law enforcement professionals who provided superior leadership, expertise, and camaraderie that resulted in a well-organized and incident-free Super Bowl.

Thank you again for the opportunity to appear before you today and for your continued support of DHS, ICE, and all the agencies that contributed to protecting the Super Bowl. I would be pleased to answer any questions.

Mrs. BROOKS. Thank you, Special Agent McLees.

The Chairwoman now recognizes Lieutenant Colonel Cetnar to testify for 5 minutes.

STATEMENT OF EDWARD CETNAR, DEPUTY SUPERINTENDENT, OPERATIONS, NEW JERSEY STATE POLICE

Lt. Col. CETNAR. Madam Chairwoman, Congressman Payne, Congressman Pascrell, let me begin by saying thank you to the Committee on Homeland Security and the subcommittee for the advocacy and support you have consistently shown to the New Jersey State Police in our pursuit for effective management and overall preparedness operations in our everyday duties and responsibility to protect and serve the citizenry of New Jersey from all crimes and all hazards.

Again, my name is Edward Cetnar, and I serve as a lieutenant colonel deputy superintendent to the Operations Branch. I am pleased to appear before the subcommittee today to highlight some of our key accomplishments of the past year and to answer questions you may have in regards to mass gathering security using our coordinated approach to Super Bowl XLVIII and other large-scale event models.

In preparation for Super Bowl XLVIII, the New Jersey State Police coordinated the activities of over 100 different Federal, State, county, and local agencies. This coordination included the development and oversight of 28 subcommittee working groups. The working groups covered the many disciplines required to secure an event of this magnitude.

The New Jersey State Police executed a plan to secure Super Bowl XLVIII using an air, land, and sea concept. This approach was the most aggressive security plan ever executed at an NFL Super Bowl. Focusing upon all manner of threats and hazards, from weather to terrorism, the New Jersey State Police developed a security plan encompassing input from the over 100 agencies that participated as a means to eliminate the threat of disruption and terrorist attack.

A broad spectrum of planning involved matters of tactical operations, cyber, intelligence, aviation, bomb detection, and emergency management, in addition to many other areas of vulnerability. In addition, the New Jersey State Police was also responsible for collaborating and coordinating security efforts with the State of New York, as well as the city of New York.

As a result of this unprecedented level of collaboration with partners from Federal, State, local, and county officials, as well as the private sector, more than 80,000 fans in attendance and more than 160 million viewers world-wide enjoyed America's premier sporting event.

The New Jersey State Police continues to establish best practices and has employed both preparedness and tactical operations that demonstrate our ability to prepare and respond to any incident or event, as well as any disaster that may impact the State of New Jersey.

I thank you for your attention today and for the opportunity to share this testimony with you, and I also would be happy to answer any questions.

[The prepared statement of Lt. Col. Cetnar follows:]

PREPARED STATEMENT OF EDWARD CETNAR

JUNE 23, 2014

Madam Chairwoman, Congressman Payne, and Members of the subcommittee: Let me begin by saying thank you to the Committee on Homeland Security and the subcommittee for the advocacy and support you have consistently shown the New Jersey State Police in our pursuit for effective management and overall preparedness operations in our everyday duties and responsibility to protect and serve the citizenry of New Jersey from all crimes, and all hazards.

My name is Edward Cetnar, and I serve as Lieutenant Colonel, Deputy Superintendent to the Operations Branch. I am pleased to appear before the subcommittee today to highlight some of our key accomplishments of the past year and to answer questions you may have in regards to "Mass Gathering Security" using our coordinated approach to Super Bowl XLVIII and other large-scale events as models.

In preparation for Super Bowl XLVIII, the New Jersey State Police coordinated the activities of over 100 different Federal, State, county, and local agencies. This coordination included the development and oversight of 28 Subcommittee Working Groups. The Working Groups covered the many disciplines required to secure an event of this magnitude.

The New Jersey State Police executed a plan to secure Super Bowl XLVIII using an air, land, and sea concept. This approach was the most aggressive security plan ever executed at an NFL Super Bowl. Focusing upon all manner of threats and hazards, from weather to terrorism, the New Jersey State Police developed a security plan encompassing input from over 100 agencies as a means to eliminate the threat of disruption and terrorist attack.

A broad spectrum of planning involved matters of tactical operations, cyber, intelligence, aviation, bomb detection, and emergency management, in addition to many other areas of vulnerability. In addition, the NJSP was also responsible for collaborating and coordinating security efforts with the State of New York, as well as New York City.

As a result of this unprecedented level of collaboration with partners from Federal, State, county, and local law enforcement and the private sector, more than 80,000 fans in attendance and more than 160 million viewers world-wide enjoyed America's premier sporting event.

The New Jersey State Police continues to establish best practices and has employed both preparedness and tactical operations that demonstrate our ability to prepare and respond to any incident, event, or disaster that may impact the State of New Jersey. I thank you for your attention today and for the opportunity to share this testimony. I would be happy to answer any questions you may have.

Mrs. BROOKS. Thank you, Lieutenant Colonel Cetnar.

The Chairwoman now recognizes Chief Koumoutsos to testify for 5 minutes.

STATEMENT OF LOUIS KOUMOUTSOS, PORT AUTHORITY PO-LICE, OFFICE OF THE PORT AUTHORITY CHIEF OF SECU-RITY, THE PORT AUTHORITY OF NEW YORK AND NEW JER-SEY

Chief KOUMOUTSOS. Good morning, Congresswoman Brooks, Congressman Payne, and Congressman Pascrell. Thank you for the opportunity to testify on behalf of the actions of the Port Authority Police relative to the Super Bowl. Good morning.

At the inception of the Super Bowl award to the New York metropolitan area, the National Football League presented the calendar of events and regional activities planned within the region for the Super Bowl XLVIII operational period. With the addition of a Homeland Security Special Event Assessment Rating Number 1 event to the metropolitan area, the Port Authority Police Department acknowledged the fact that the security and operational challenges faced would be substantial to the region and the Port Authority in specific.

Principal law enforcement agencies began partnerships to regionalize and coordinate security efforts and operational deployment initiatives to achieve an overarching security strategy to support the Super Bowl event.

The New Jersey State Police, the New York City Police Department, New Jersey Transit Police Department, the Federal Bureau of Investigation, the Port Authority Police Department, and other local and Federal partners created numerous subcommittees to support the subdivisions of each event security component. Law enforcement, private business, public utility, transportation facility operations personnel, and other public safety components were assembled to support the regional Super Bowl security strategy.

All interagency subcommittees reported progress and initiatives to the overarching security committees, which were tasked with command and control and the coordination of the subgroups. The Port Authority Police provided representation for each of the aforementioned interagency subcommittees throughout the Super Bowl XLVIII security planning process.

Examples of some established interagency subcommittees included: Aviation subcommittees, tasked with the security strategy, operational support, and passenger management at all regional major airports; interagency communication subcommittees, tasked with the coordination of interoperability radio networks to facilitate the missions of the numerous security details and escort personnel; dignitary/VIP and escort subcommittees, tasked with the interagency coordination of dignitaries and VIPs traversing Hudson River crossings and inter-State facilities. We also have the explosive device response and hazardous material mitigation. They were tasked with the interagency coordinated efforts for Special Operations Division resources to avoid redundancy of asset deployment, and to facilitate the overarching hazardous material mitigation footprint of the region.

In addition to the interagency security subcommittees, the Port Authority Police created intra-agency law enforcement, facility operations, and security department subcommittees to address specific events and impacts to Port Authority facilities throughout the Super Bowl operational period.

Daily manpower deployment strategies were created specific to Port Authority facility needs based on sanctioned and unsanctioned Super Bowl events. Table-top exercises and information-gathering sessions across Port Authority line departments were created to facilitate business continuity planning in an effort to mitigate operational impacts in the event a facility vital to a specific Super Bowl event was inoperable due to unforeseen circumstances.

Upon completion of the planning stages in support of the event, the Port Authority Police Department and the Port Authority Office of Emergency Management took the lead in coordinating information sharing and dissemination across Port Authority line departments and facility operations personnel. The information gathered during subcommittee participation was compiled and correlated for each operational period to assess specific facility impact and establish a gauge for logistical support needed. Meetings were prompted with key affected facility personnel to develop strategies to mitigate security concerns, increase police patrol volume, and identify staffing issues.

For example, based on regional events scheduled in support of the Super Bowl, PATH operations increased train activity on the system to accommodate the anticipated increased volume of patrons to the Super Bowl Boulevard event in the Times Square area. Weekend schedules were suspended over the Super Bowl weekend, and additional personnel were assigned accordingly at PATH Station locations. Emergency equipment was pre-staged and available for rapid response in the event of an emergency within the PATH system.

The Lincoln Tunnel facility reversed rush hour configurations on Super Bowl Sunday to support the travel routes of the host committee-sponsored Motor Coach transportation vehicles and et cetera. Partnered with the New York City Police Department, the Port Authority Police Department was strategically deployed along the bus routes to support the altered ingress and egress routes created at the Lincoln Tunnel Command.

Prior to the identification of the Super Bowl game participants, all major airports developed a detailed security deployment strategy to accommodate the perceived passenger activities during the Super Bowl operational period. Upon the identification of the volume of general aviation activity at Teterboro Airport and the participating teams' decision to utilize Newark Airport, several operational meetings were held to coordinate and facilitate the Port Authority Police and the Newark Airport operations community, which resulted in comprehensive planning to support the participating teams' arrivals and departures.

Tenant information was solicited inside the New Jersey Marine Terminal community to track Class 7 radiological and hazardous material shipment activity traversing roadways in proximity to Super Bowl events.

Information sharing was initiated with supporting agencies in the Teterboro area via the Transportation Subcommittee to meet the challenges that were often faced by the increased VIP activity exiting and entering the facility during the operational period. Special security provisions were made utilizing designated parking areas at Newark Airport for the volumes of staged hired vehicles contracted for spectator transportation.

Technological efforts have the following. The Port Authority Police Technical Services Division was solicited to support the Port Authority Police PAPD throughout the Super Bowl operational period. Camera view links were provided from the tunnels, bridges, and terminal, and PATH facilities for real-time situational awareness inside the PATC Emergency Operations Center. Camera views were shared with partner agencies at the New Jersey State Police Command Center within the American Dream Complex, the New Jersey Department of Transportation Operations Center, and the FBI IOC, which was located in Newark.

Early in the interagency coordination process, the identification was made for interoperable communication networks in the Communication subcommittee meetings. Radio interoperability patches across State lines were to support the VIP escort mission during the Super Bowl operational period. All planned patches were tested at great length prior to implementation and utilization. The networks performed superbly, and interagency coordination of effort was achieved via utilization of the interoperable radio communications framework.

In closing, the security deployment strategy generated in support of the Super Bowl event was a major success. I would like to thank the regional partners for all their efforts and hard work in all phases of planning and operations in support of the Super Bowl XLVIII event.

Thank you.

[The prepared statement of Chief Koumoutsos follows:]

PREPARED STATEMENT OF LOUIS KOUMOUTSOS

JUNE 23, 2014

Good morning, at the inception of the Super Bowl Award to the New York Metropolitan area, the National Football League presented the calendar of events and regional activities planned within the region for the Super Bowl 48 Operational Period. With the addition of a Homeland Security Special Event Assessment Rating No. 1 event to the metropolitan area, The Port Authority Police Department acknowledged the fact that the security and operational challenges faced would be substantial to the region and the Port Authority in specific.

Principal Law Enforcement agencies began partnerships to regionally coordinate security efforts and operational deployment initiatives to achieve an over-arching security strategy to support the Super Bowl Event.

The New Jersey State Police, the New York City Police Department, New Jersey Transit Police Department, The Federal Bureau of Investigation, the Port Authority Police Department, and other local and Federal partners created numerous subcommittees to support the subdivisions of each event security component. Law enforcement, private business, public utility, transportation facility operations personnel, and other public safety components were assembled to support the regional Super Bowl Security strategy. All inter-agency subcommittees reported progress and initiatives to the over-arching steering committees, which were tasked with command and control, and the coordination of the sub-groups. The Port Authority Police provided representation for each of the aforementioned inter-agency subcommittees throughout the Super Bowl XLVIII (48) security planning process.

Examples of established inter-agency subcommittees included:

Aviation Subcommittees

Tasked with the security strategy, operational support, and passenger management at all regional major airports.

Inter-Agency Communication Subcommittees

Tasked with the coordination of inter-operability radio networks to facilitate the missions of the numerous security details and escort personnel.

Dignitary/VIP/Escorts Subcommittees

Tasked with the inter-agency coordination of dignitaries and VIPs traversing Hudson River crossings and inter-State facilities.

EXPLOSIVE DEVICE RESPONSE & HAZARDOUS MATERIAL MITIGATION

Tasked with the inter-agency coordinated efforts for Special Operations Division resources, to avoid redundancy of asset deployment, and the facilitate the over-arching hazardous material mitigation footprint of the region.

In addition to the inter-agency security sub-committees, the Port Authority Police created intra-agency law enforcement, facility operations, and security department subcommittees to address specific events and impacts to Port Authority facilities throughout the Super Bowl Operational period.

- Daily Manpower deployment strategies were created specific to Port Authority Facility needs based on Sanctioned and Unsanctioned Super Bowl Events.
- Table-top exercises and information-gathering sessions across Port Authority Line Departments were created to facilitate business continuity planning, in an effort to mitigate operational impacts in the event a facility vital to a specific Super Bowl event was inoperable due to unforeseen circumstances.

Upon completion of the planning stages in support of the event, The Port Authority Police Department and the Port Authority Office of Emergency Management took the lead in coordinating information sharing and dissemination across Port Authority line departments and facility operations personnel. The information gathered during subcommittee participation was compiled and correlated for each operational period to assess specific facility impact, and establish a gauge for logistical support needed. Meetings were prompted with key affected facility personnel to develop strategies to mitigate security concerns, increase police patrol volume, and identify staffing issues.

For example:

Based on regional events scheduled in support of the Super Bowl, PATH operations increased train activity on the system to accommodate the anticipated increased volume of patrons to the Super Bowl Boulevard Event in the Times Square area. Weekend schedules were suspended over the Super Bowl weekend, and additional personnel were assigned accordingly at PATH Station locations. Emergency equipment was pre-staged and available for rapid response in the event of an emergency within the PATH system.

The Lincoln Tunnel facility reversed rush hour configurations on Super Bowl Sunday to support the travel routes of the Host Committee sponsored Motor Coach transportation vehicles. Partnered with the New York City Police Department, the Port Authority Police Department was strategically deployed along the bus routes to support the altered ingress and egress routes created at the Lincoln Tunnel Command.

Prior to the identification of the Super Bowl game participants, all major airports developed a detailed security deployment strategy to accommodate the perceived passenger activities during the Super Bowl XLVIII Operational period. Upon the identification of the volume of general aviation activity at Teterboro Airport, and the participating team's decision to utilize Newark Airport, several operational meeting and coordination efforts were facilitated by the Port Authority Police and the Newark Airport operations community, resulting in comprehensive planning to support the participating team's arrivals and departures.

Tennant information was solicited inside the New Jersey Marine Terminal community to track Class 7 Radiological and other hazardous material shipment activity traversing roadways in proximity to Super Bowl 48 events.

Information sharing was initiated with supporting agencies in the Teterboro area via the transportation subcommittee, to meet the challenges faced by the increased VIP activity exiting and entering the facility during the operational period. Special security provisions were made utilizing designated parking areas at Newark Airport for the volumes of staged hired vehicles contracted for spectator transportation.

Technological Efforts

The Port Authority Police Technical Services Division was solicited to support the Port Authority Police PAPD throughout the Super Bowl Operational Period. Camera view links were provided from The Tunnels Bridges and Terminal and PATH facilities for real-time situational awareness inside the PATC Emergency Operations Center. Camera views were shared with partner agencies at the New Jersey State Police Command Center within the American Dream Complex, The New Jersey Department of Transportation Operations Center, and the FBI IOC in Newark.

Early in the inter-agency coordination process, the identification was made for inter-operable communication networks in the communication subcommittee meetings. Radio inter-operability patches across State lines to support the VIP escort mission during the Super Bowl Operational Period were created. All planned patches were tested at great length prior to implementation, and utilization. The networks performed superbly, and inter-agency coordination of effort was achieved via utilization of the inter-operable radio communications framework.

In closing, the Security Deployment strategy generated in support of the Super Bowl Event was a major success. I would like to thank the regional partners for all their efforts and hard work in all phases of planning and operations in support of the Super Bowl XLVIII (48) event. Thank you.

Mrs. BROOKS. Thank you, Chief.

I now recognize Chief Centanni for 5 minutes of testimony.

STATEMENT OF JOHN G. CENTANNI, FIRE CHIEF, FIRE DEPARTMENT, CITY OF NEWARK, NEW JERSEY

Chief CENTANNI. Yes, Madam Chairwoman, Ranking Member and Congressman. First I would like to thank you for having the

Fire Service here and having a voice in these hearings, which I think is a very important step moving forward in that communication sharing.

Newark Fire Department has a unique role in the region, being the largest fire department in the State and one of the largest givers of mutual aid and partners throughout the region. So in preparation and training for the Super Bowl event, the city of Newark Fire Department attended multiple meetings over several months with Federal, State, county, and local agencies, both on the public and private-sector side, including the Meadowlands Fire Department, in an effort to fully understand the scope of this event and the potential concerns and impacts that it would have on the region, and more specifically on the city of Newark in regards to fire service preparedness and operational concerns.

Based upon information and lessons learned through early meetings, the Newark Fire Department, in coordination with the Division of Fire Safety and New Jersey Homeland Security office, and our county and regional coordinators, prepared an overall operation and response plan to strategically deploy assets throughout a coordinated response effort. Areas that were highlighted during our early meetings were familiarization training and drills for large hazardous material and decontamination of events. Potential areas of concern were also the marine area waterway events, and we worked alongside the United States Coast Guard, State Police, and our other regional fire department marine divisions to assure that we had an operational plan in place for such an event.

We also worked closely with our USAR, Urban Search Area Rescue Strike Team and New Jersey Task Force 1 in multiple planning, training, and preparedness events. Our code enforcement fire prevention office engaged in early pre-planning of areas that would be of concern for large gatherings and to be prepared for that type of venue.

Interoperability and communications and preparedness for this event, the city of Newark Fire Department worked closely with Federal, State, county, and local agencies once again, as well as the Department of Homeland Security, to ensure radio communication and interoperability frequencies throughout all disciplines—i.e., fire, EMS, law enforcement—were achieved. Through various subcommittees made up of many of the aforementioned agencies, interoperability was achieved by testing involving mutual drills, formalized radio communication testing procedures, and actual sharing of equipment—i.e., portable radios, et cetera.

An area of specific highlight for the city of Newark Fire Department was the mutual link capability which allowed us to stream real-time video information and audio information to the Command Center at the East Rutherford MetLife Stadium, as well as the New Jersey Rock and our OEM Center in Newark. I think that was quite helpful in showing the interoperability and capability of the fire side with the law enforcement partners.

Overall, the Newark Fire Department, as I stated earlier, plays a unique role in the region, from preparing, training, interoperability communication response functions, to potential incidents and events could have occurred, specific infrastructure and points of concern of target areas for Newark—Newark Airport, Penn Station, waterways, multiple highways, Prudential Arena where we had the Super Bowl Media Day. So these were all areas of concern where we had to pre-plan, pre-stage, and work drills out that we were prepared to respond in a supporting role with the law enforcement agencies.

As the largest fire department in the area, I said it already, we have a unique role in being partners with all of our surrounding communities. Also noted in a cooperative effort, the Newark Fire Department, Patterson Fire Department were representing one of the USAR Strike Team agencies and the New Jersey National Guard Weapons of Mass Destruction Civil Support Team were embedded in Newark and prepared to respond as a task force to not only Newark but the entire region, if needed.

Lessons learned for us in the Newark Fire Department. Overall information sharing and communication through the meetings and preparedness with the planning committee, law enforcement, and the fire service greatly improved throughout the process of the Super Bowl planning event. Early on, the fire department may have not been as engaged as they were later into the process, and I think that was a direct result of the partnerships coming together and very important to keep that moving forward.

It is my opinion that continuing with that good effort of information sharing, multiple agency discipline training, drills, and functional operational plans as a united front will definitely strengthen the security efforts of any large-scale events, whether it be here in our region or anywhere across the country, and that would work in the truest sense of a united incident command front.

Thank you.

Mrs. BROOKS. Thank you, Chief.

At this time, I will now recognize myself for 5 minutes of questioning.

This is really a question for all of you. As you worked to prepare for Super Bowl XLVIII, I am curious how you engaged with officials and public safety officials, first responders from prior venues. How did you learn about what it would take to put on a successful Super Bowl and keeping it safe? Are you working with next year's officials? So how is it that you worked with the prior year officials, and what kind of work are you doing with future Super Bowl officials, because obviously the Super Bowls are set for several years to come.

Does anyone want to start us out?

Mr. McLEES. The Federal coordinator, there is a continuity that takes place, that has since 2001. The coordination team is usually appointed from, again, the local jurisdiction, and it is diverse in the sense that it was myself from the Secret Service, as well as a representative from NPPD, and critical infrastructure. So we were able to work with the past year's Federal coordination teams, and they sort-of showed us the ropes; and then, of course, we went to New Orleans the year before to watch it put into action. Just to add to that the point about the diversity of the team, working with the State Police, understanding the Federal resources that were out there, the spectrum of Federal resources that were available. We came from different places, so we had different viewpoints of how we could help and where we could find those resources.

Mrs. BROOKS. Had you been a Federal coordinator before prior to this incident?

Mr. MCLEES. No, this was the first time.

Mrs. BROOKS. Or this event?

Mr. MCLEES. This was the first time.

Mrs. BROOKS. So the different Federal agencies that you coordinated with, approximately how many were there?

Mr. MCLEES. Over 30.

Mrs. BROOKS. So did you have separate meetings from, say, New Jersey State Police, or coordinating the Federal resources? Because I know even within the Department of Homeland Security, that can be a challenge.

Mr. MCLEES. It was, and we did have DHS meetings in support of the effort where we would make sure that we understood everything that was there to offer, as well as the other agencies, and there were many, from DHS, HHS, DOJ, DOD. I mean, it was the alphabet in terms of support.

Mrs. BROOKS. Lieutenant Colonel.

Lt. Col. CETNAR. From a New Jersey State Police perspective, what we did was the same as the Federal Government. We attended both the Super Bowl and the prior one in New Orleans to basically get their practices and best practices as to how they approached the Super Bowl. As you know, the Indy Super Bowl and the New Orleans Super Bowl are quite different from the New Jersey Super Bowl. Just the land structure alone and what we are surrounded by, we are not embedded into a city, brought a number of different challenges to us, as well as the proximity to New York City and the constant threat in this region of terrorism kind of brought a whole different host of issues for New Jersey to see.

So what we did early on, working very closely with the NFL, was we developed our subcommittees. As we moved on, our subcommittees grew, as I testified, up to 28. What we did is, when we traveled to both venues, we had the folks that I put in charge of these different subcommittees. They would embed themselves with the folks in the departments of Indy, whether it was emergency management, police, tactical air operations, cyber intelligence, as well as New Orleans, and they mirrored those folks for the entire time we were there.

Then on game day itself, they would observe the operations that were going on at both Super Bowls to bring back those best practices to New Jersey to sit with myself, as well as the FCO, and we would come up with our diverse plan for the New Jersey Super Bowl and the challenges that we were going to have.

In addition to that, not only members of the New Jersey State Police but some of our partnering agencies, New Jersey Transit, Port Authority, all sent folks and bought into the concept that we started right from the beginning, taken our advisement from NFL as to what would work and what needed to be done in order to do a successful planning concept for this Super Bowl.

So it was very worthwhile for us to do that, as well as our Super Bowl, we hosted Phoenix as well as Santa Clara to come in to see what we did here.

So it is a partnership that continues from venue to venue, and everything that we have we are now offering to our future Super

Bowl hosts to make sure that if there were best practices that we used here that worked, or if there were some other issues that maybe we would have done differently, we are getting ahead of that and making sure that they know that so they can make sure that they can have a very successful and safe Super Bowl also.

Mrs. BROOKS. Thank you.

Would any others like to comment?

Chief.

Chief KOUMOUTSOS. Yes. As the Lieutenant Colonel mentioned here, when this thing started 18 months ago and we started talking about the concept and the event coming into this region here, most of us, if not all the agencies that were involved, usually have a major event. We have New Year's Eve and several other venues that we are used to and that form themselves into this area quite frequently.

The one thing that we have learned over time is communications, talking to each other, talking to the other agencies, having a Plan B, having a Plan C, what if, what if, the equipment, the radiological detectors that I testified to, and so many other resources and equipment that was used and deployed that can give us a heads-up, if you will, ahead of time, so this way we can react.

The fact of the matter that we came together with other agencies and we used the patching technique, which allows multiple agencies to come together and talk on one frequency, enabled us to have the same message out there if something were to happen. We had a business continuity plan in place. We had other means in place. We had the harbor. We had the air covered. We had the tunnels covered. We had rapid deployment teams and strike teams.

So we were certainly ready, and we were capable, and we were impressed with some of the drills, because we did exercise frequently during the off hours when people were not alarmed, and we would put something out to the public and advise that we are doing drills and we are planning.

But really, the core mission of these drills was to understand the reality of it if something were to come up and how it would be handled.

The other thing is, with all the officers out there, they got to meet each other. So if something did happen, they were able to interact, be it the fire department, the State police, the Federal agencies, the local agencies. So I do recall at the conclusion, which was late that morning, the next morning I should say, I did notice a lot of officers patting each other on the back for a job well done, and that is what it is about.

Mrs. BROOKS. Terrific. Thank you.

Okay, thank you. I'm sorry, my time is up.

I now would turn it over to Congressman Payne for 5 minutes of questioning.

Mr. PAYNE. Thank you, Madam Chairwoman.

This question is for all the witnesses. In the year leading up to the Super Bowl, we saw the Boston Marathon bombings devastate those participating in and watching the race. In the months leading up to the Olympics in Sochi, suicide bombings tore through mass transit sites in Russia. We had a committee hearing last week on first responders and lessons learned, and I just want to once again commend the officials in the Boston area that handled that situation that day.

We found out that the scene for the most critically injured at the Boston Marathon were Medevac'd out of there within 22 minutes of the bombing, which I felt was absolutely incredible to coordinate that effort and get the most severely wounded on the way to the hospital, that scene clear with the most injured within 22 minutes.

So my question is: What changes, if any, did you make to your security planning after the Boston bombings to address the threat of attacks of mass transit during the Super Bowl?

Mr. McLees.

Mr. McLEES. From the mass transit perspective, there were a lot of policies put in place by the NFL which changed the way that people entered the stadium, and it was the clear bag policy—no backpacks—and essentially pushing that opportunity further and further away from the stadium, and that was put into place in the mass transit system as well.

Again, from the Federal perspective, the assets that we offered to assist in that system were—the rail link between Secaucus Junction and New Jersey Transit at the stadium, we added TSA assets there to assist them in screening bags before they left to get inside that perimeter.

Lt. Col. CETNAR. As you alluded to, the trains and mass transit system, and this Super Bowl being deemed the mass transit Super Bowl, bringing folks from 2 weeks prior, we didn't know where they were coming from, had they ever been to New York City, ever been to New Jersey. These posed great concerns to us and how we were going to move people safely.

Chief Trucillo of New Jersey Transit was embedded with us right from the start from a planning concept. So as we discussed, we had air, land, and sea concept. The water-borne issue was because of the proximity to the water surrounding MetLife Stadium. That was a law enforcement issue. But the trains and buses, how we enhanced some of the issues of package screening, as well as behavioral science techniques to make sure we used everything possible to prevent any disruption of the event or somebody disrupting the buses or the rail system.

TSA was a huge partner with us, and Mr. McLees was one of the partners that made that possible for us to use the TSA screeners, as well as some of the folks that we trained using DHS funding from behavioral science using Patriot training. These were huge things that a lot of our troopers, hundreds of troopers were trained in behavioral analysis to hopefully detect disruptive behavior that was going on, or if somebody wanted to infiltrate the Super Bowl or mass transit system to cause disruption. We used this concept throughout the NFL season, and unlike any other venue throughout the country, MetLife Stadium has a game every week because we host two teams. So we had a lot of practice in exercising throughout the season using the techniques and some of the rail practices and screenings throughout the year.

So we rehearsed for 16 weeks about training some of the things that we wanted to leading up to Super Bowl Sunday. As you know, it was very successful because there was no disruption to the Super Bowl, and it was because of the coordinated efforts between the law enforcement agencies that were brought together and how we seamlessly made sure that there was transparency in communication and everything that we had to do, and that was critical.

Anything that I had as a concern, I needed to share that with every one of our partners out there to make sure if they had information that came back to me and it was operated and communicated out of one location, so everybody was sharing real-time information.

Chief KOUMOUTSOS. Good morning, sir. Leading to the event, going back a little bit, there are some things that we do deploy on a daily basis because of the number of folks that we have traversing through our facilities. One of the things that we use is what we call a bag check, where we go through the bags of certain people through a sequence number, and that was intensified during the Super Bowl week and that weekend.

The step-on/step-off concept, where we step on the trains with officers with heavy weapons, we look around, and we step off, not delaying the train, of course, but it takes less than 30 seconds. The same thing with the buses at our bus depots, at the bus station. At the George Washington Bridge, same concept.

At the airports on arrival, officers meeting airplanes, officers down at the arrivals area with heavy weapons, just looking, using the Patriot training, behavioral assessment, some of the tools that we used and that we currently use every day. We just expanded it by a few hours, and that is 12 hours in total because we prepared before and we prepared after.

The super searches. What does that mean? Officers go and enforce, go through a station or a bus depot and a heavy presence used, and the radiological pagers, the backpacks and so on. Multiple agency super searches where we get multiple agencies in New York City where we do backpack assessments, we do checks of various stations and so on. So this is a big, big thing that we do in the tri-State—actually, in New York City.

And, of course, the technology that we use.

Chief CENTANNI. Congressman, on the response side for the Fire Service, it is always in a supporting role to one of these events, or more so in a supporting role, although we did learn the lessons that we can be there in a preventive role also. But as we referenced to the event, I think some of the lessons learned, the boots on the ground, the relationships, that relationships that we built with the State Police and all of our agencies that are here now are important, and they are so important to the fact of, as we speak, we have multiple Federal and State agencies doing joint training with our Special Operations Division in Newark based on what they have learned from the inter-cooperation and interoperability that we saw during the Super Bowl, and I believe that that really makes that Boston scenario work when you come together at that scene. You have the relationships. You already have the technology put in place to make a nice, cohesive response.

Mr. PAYNE. Thank you, sir.

I yield back.

Mrs. BROOKS. Thank you.

The Chairwoman now recognizes the gentleman from New Jersey, Mr. Pascrell, for 5 minutes of questioning.

Mr. PASCRELL. Thank you.

Critical to any implementation of communication and interoperability, we saw what a disaster that was on 9/11, so let's focus now on our own period of time here. How would you rank, on a scale of 1 to 5, 5 being the best, the communications and interoperability that each of you participated in at the Super Bowl? I want you to be as frank as possible, 1 to 5.

Mr. MCLEES. I would say it was a 5. The DHS—there was a subcommittee on communications interoperability that supplied personnel from the District of Columbia, as well as my agency, and from my experiences there were no problems with communications in the week-and-a-half, 2 weeks operational period leading up to the event.

Mr. PASCRELL. Lieutenant Colonel, you talked about the multiple agencies involved here, a lot of agencies, so I am anxious to hear what you have to say about that.

Lt. Col. CETNAR. Sir, you know, the months after the Super Bowl, as I have been speaking to a lot of different folks about how we did this, how we put this together, communications—I will go with the interoperability part first. I had that as a 5. It was a very complex plan that we had to put together. When you are dealing with over 100 different agencies, as well as communicating with the private sector, four counties in New Jersey, four towns in New Jersey, the State of New York, New York City, our Federal partners, it goes on and on and on, to tie all of them in to where we had our command post, as well as the Rock, the FBI, those were monumental concerns of ours, how we were going to communicate, and God forbid we had an incident, that everything was going to continue on to us doing our next steps with search and rescue, recovery, as well as dealing with a potential crime scene if, in fact, we were attacked.

From that standpoint, the interoperability I thought was very seamless, and let me step back to the other issue of communication. Having over 100 different agencies, as well as private-sector folks in New York and New Jersey informed as to what was going to happen the week leading up to the Super Bowl, as well as Super Bowl Sunday, when we developed our subcommittees, as I said, we had up to 28 of them, one of the best things that we did in New Jersey right from the start was once we identified our chairs and co-chairs, which was usually a New Jersey State Trooper commander or someone from the Federal side or, if it didn't apply, the fire side, the experts that needed to do that because obviously the State Police was not going to dictate what Fire needed to do, that was their expertise, but they were embedded into the system with us and the subcommittees.

We started briefings every 30 days. Now, you would think 18 months out, 2 years out, folks every 30 days we had to brief out, it worked, because after 30 days, if you had an issue, no matter what the agency was, you only had 30 days to deal with that, and once you brought it to myself and the other commanders that were there, we then, if we had to take it to the executive level folks, which were the heads of the other agencies——

Mr. PASCRELL. So you would give it a 5, too?

Lt. Col. CETNAR. I would give it a 5, and I thought it was absolutely seamless.

Mr. PASCRELL. How about you, Chief?

Chief KOUMOUTSOS. Sir, I would give it a 5. We started early, as the Lieutenant Colonel mentioned. We had the opportunity to have several drills, communication drills with the other agencies. One thing I want to bring out is the fact that we had over 100 VIP movements through the Lincoln Tunnel within a 2-hour window.

Mr. PASCRELL. What are VIP movements?

Chief KOUMOUTSOS. The teams had their officials coming through the hotels in New York and the Boulevard. They were——

Mr. PASCRELL. Was that a distraction for you to do your job?

Chief KOUMOUTSOS. No, no, because it was all sequenced and everything was planned out properly. That took several agencies—NYPD, PAPD, and other folks, the Weehawken guys.

Mr. PASCRELL. Did you communicate to the Fire Department?

Chief KOUMOUTSOS. They were with us, sir. They were with us the entire time. We had a truck actually standing by right outside the Lincoln Tunnel, and one on the other side, on the New York side. We had tow trucks in place. We were communicating with them in the event we had a disabled vehicle in the tunnel. So it was flawless. It worked. The drills leading up to the event worked. I had two great lieutenants here behind me that were behind the whole process and they kept me informed, and we kept on pushing because, you know what? Everybody needed to know what everybody was doing.

Mr. PASCRELL. Chief, you know what happened on 9/11, and other things since.

Chief CENTANNI. Yes.

Mr. PASCRELL. Our Fire Department was in left field, and public safety, the rest of public safety was in right field. How has that changed in terms of this past example of this mass gathering?

Chief CENTANNI. I think what the Super Bowl showed us, it can be done. Through these subcommittees, the drills, the training, the sharing of equipment, it happened. It happened flawlessly. Would that happen right now if we go to an event? I am not as confident as that day, but I would defer to what I heard here today. When you talk about a 5, I was in shock. My biggest concern was communication, especially coming from the fire side, being able to communicate with law enforcement. Through the commitments of the State Police releasing certain frequencies, the coordination of all of the agencies, assuring that everyone was able to communicate, it was unbelievable, and I was very impressed with it. We need to be able to do that on a daily basis.

Mr. PASCRELL. Madam Chairwoman, I am very impressed with the responses. I can't stay for the entire hearing, but I want these guys to know, you gentlemen to know that we want to be helpful to you because you have situations that you cannot, within your own agency, solve. So if we can't be of any help, then we shouldn't be here. So we want to know this. I am sure I speak for the Chairwoman and Mr. Payne. As to any information you can give to us during this hearing, whether it be Panel 1 or Panel 2 as to what would you have changed, would you have changed anything? Now, if you are telling me you wouldn't have changed anything, then I know something is wrong. So that is why we are here, and thank each of you for your testimony. Thank you.

Mrs. BROOKS. Thank you very much, Congressman, for that very important line of questioning, and I would like to reiterate what the really senior Member of Congress here is sharing with us. That is why we are here, to learn from you as well, and for us to be resources for you. I just would like to commend all of you for your valuable testimony. I would like to also commend my former colleague at the Justice Department, your Governor, Governor Christi and Governor Cuomo and the mayors who worked on this, those who lead your agencies, for such an outstanding job in governing over such an incredible event. So I just want to thank you all.

The record will be open for up to 10 days. Normally we might have another line of questioning, but we have a very important second panel, and so we might be submitting other questions to you. So the record will remain open, and you can respond in writing if you should receive any other questions.

So at this time, you are now dismissed, and we will just take a very brief break. I want to thank you all so very much for your time, and I appreciate your outstanding work.

Mr. PAYNE. Madam Chairwoman, just before we break up, I wasn't going to do this, but I think there is a gentleman in the audience that has played a vital role in Newark doing the job that it has done so far in terms of OEM and homeland security, and that is Keith Isaacs, who is our director here in Newark. The Rock is a great place, but you have to come to Newark to see our facility. It is first class. We are very proud of the work that he is doing every day. Thank you.

Mrs. BROOKS. Thank you.

This panel is now dismissed, and the Clerk will prepare the witness table for our second panel.

[Recess.]

Mrs. BROOKS. I would like to welcome everyone on our second panel to today's hearing, and thank you for your participation.

At this time, Ranking Member Congressman Payne is going to introduce parts of our panel.

Mr. PAYNE. Thank you, Madam Chairwoman.

Mr. Dan Grossi is the director of event security for the National Football League, a position he has held since January 2011. In this capacity, he is responsible for the planning and implementation of security at all major NFL events, including the Super Bowl and the NFL draft. Mr. Grossi has previously served as the NFL Security Representative in Tampa, Florida, with the Tampa Police Department, and with the United States Capitol Police.

Mr. Daniel DeLorenzi is the director of safety and security services at MetLife Stadium, a position he has held since 2009. In this position, he is responsible for creating and implementing emergency operation plans and coordinating State and security operations with law enforcement, the fire department, and EMS. Prior to this position, he has served as the director of security for Bank of America and was the deputy chief of police for the Police Department in Newark, New Jersey.

Wow, I had a tough time with that one.

I yield to the gentlelady.

Mrs. BROOKS. Thank you.

At this time, I would like to welcome my constituent, Mr. Doug Boles, who is serving as president of the Indianapolis Motor Speedway since July 2013, previously serving as the Speedway's vice president of communications. He has also worked in the Indiana House of Representatives, and we both worked for former mayor of Indianapolis, Steve Goldsmith. He served as director of governmental and corporate affairs for the city of Indianapolis.

I want to welcome you to New Jersey.

Mr. PAYNE. Then we have Dr. Fred Roberts. He is the director of the Command, Control, and Interoperability Center for Advanced Data Analysis at Rutgers University and Department of Homeland Security Center of Excellence. He is also a distinguished professor of mathematics and serves as the director emeritus and senior advisor of the Center for Discrete Mathematics and Theoretical Computer Science. He has completed research related to stadium security, container inspection at ports, sensor management for nuclear materials detection, and the early warning of disease outbreaks in bioterrorism events.

Mrs. BROOKS. I was pleased to learn, actually, that Purdue's Homeland Security Center of Excellence is a partner of your university, and so pleased that Indiana and New Jersey are working together on homeland security issues beyond our work together.

The witnesses' full written statements—I want to thank you all for your written statements—will appear in the record.

The Chairwoman now recognizes Mr. Grossi for 5 minutes of testimony.

STATEMENT OF DAN GROSSI, DIRECTOR, EVENT SECURITY, NATIONAL FOOTBALL LEAGUE

Mr. GROSSI. Madam Chairwoman Brooks, Ranking Member Payne, Member Pascrell, and Members of the subcommittee, thank you for inviting me here to testify today. My name is Dan Grossi. I am the director of special event security for the National Football League. I appreciate the opportunity to be here and offer testimony. I hope that the NFL's successful experiences in working with a number of different public safety organizations to ensure the security of its games can be a model for similar high-profile mass gatherings.

The Super Bowl is one of our Nation's classic mass gatherings. The League sets out to strike an appropriate balance, ensuring that fans enjoy a rich and festive in-stadium experience while making their safety and security paramount. At Super Bowl XLVIII, MetLife Stadium hosted 82,000 fans in addition to 10,000 vendors, staff, and members of the National and international media. Additionally, 112 million people watched the game on television. The week leading up to the game, tens of thousands of people attended official Super Bowl events at several locations in New York and New Jersey.

Ensuring a safe and successful outcome at such a huge undertaking requires significant advance preparation and cooperation between a number of stakeholders including Federal, State, and local agencies, as well as other public and private interests.

The NFL does not create the security plan for Super Bowls. That is the role of law enforcement and other public safety organizations. Instead, the NFL is a resource for these organizations, focusing on helping them with coordination and offering them insights based on experience.

The NFL normally begins planning for Super Bowl security about a year before the game and meeting with public safety officials and discussing broad plans. For Super Bowl XLVIII, we started our planning meetings about 2 years in advance of the game based on the request of the New Jersey State Police. At these early meetings, we work on the basics of the security plan; for instance, determining which organization is responsible for which aspects of Super Bowl security.

We hold a planning meeting in April, a full production meeting in June, another planning meeting in October, and a final production meeting in December. During the time leading up to the game, the group runs countless simulations of possible security events. In addition to other security planners, I will generally attend five or six regular-season games at the host stadium. These visits give us a first-hand look at the stadium in use and occupied by fans. Again, each Super Bowl is a unique event depending on a variety of factors, some of which can be discovered only by on-scene experience.

The lead planning organizations also depend on circumstances for the particular Super Bowl. Super Bowl XLVIII, although the game was held at MetLife Stadium in New Jersey, a significant number of events, including the week-long Super Bowl Boulevard event, were held in New York City. So the New Jersey State Police and the NYPD shared the responsibility as co-leads. Public safety organizations from surrounding jurisdictions assisted with game-day security.

When the game is being held in a smaller jurisdiction with a smaller law enforcement agency, the coordination is generally done by a coalition of law enforcement agencies to support the game. This is the case for Super Bowl 50, the 2016 Super Bowl which is held at Levi Stadium, the San Francisco 49ers' home stadium located in Santa Clara, California. The Santa Clara Police Department will be the lead agency and will receive significant support from other public safety organizations and surrounding jurisdictions.

A number of Federal agencies also play an integral role in preparing and implementing the security plan. The FBI, the Department of Homeland Security, and the Secret Service are resources for the NFL and our public safety partners. They provide valuable intelligence and expertise in Super Bowl planning. The FBI works with State and local law enforcement and other Federal agencies to run background checks on the staff that will be working the Super Bowl. Customs and Border Protection, CBP, is also involved in the security plan and is responsible for searching and screening vehicles that come within the Super Bowl secure perimeter. The U.S. Postal Service is responsible for screening mail. The FAA issues a temporary flight restriction for the event which restricts aircraft from flying in close proximity to the Super Bowl.

Our goal with all the advanced planning is to ensure that everything goes as planned, while at the same time planning for any eventuality. It is absolutely vital that every organization knows its role and responsibilities, and that information is shared among the organizations seamlessly and in real time.

To help facilitate this cooperation and communication, senior officials from all of the stakeholders remain in the command post throughout the event.

As mentioned, the TFR protects the stadium perimeter by air, which is an extremely important component of Super Bowl security. For Super Bowl XLVIII game day, the FAA issued two TFRs. The first one began at noon for a 1-mile nautical ring around MetLife Stadium. No flights other than law enforcement flights are allowed in this 1-mile ring. The second TFR began at 5:00 p.m. The CBP and, if necessary, the Air Force are responsible for enforcing the TFR. TFRs are very important for helping to ensure the security for all Super Bowl games and events.

Of course, this is just a brief summary of the massive undertaking that is securing the Super Bowl. Success requires the cooperation of and coordination with numerous organizations and countless people.

The NFL is very thankful for the assistance of our Federal, State, and local partners, and we hope that we can continue to be a resource to them. Thank you again for the opportunity to testify today on such an important issue to the National Football League and the Nation. I look forward to your questions.

[The prepared statement of Mr. Grossi follows:]

PREPARED STATEMENT OF DAN GROSSI

JUNE 23, 2014

Madam Chairwoman, Ranking Member Payne, Members of the subcommittee, thank you for inviting me here to testify today. My name is Dan Grossi. I am the director of special events security for the National Football League. I appreciate the opportunity to be here and offer testimony. I hope that the NFL's successful experiences in working with a number of different public safety organizations to ensure the security of its games can be a model for similar high-profile mass gatherings.

The Super Bowl is one of our Nation's archetypical mass gatherings. The league sets out to strike an appropriate balance, ensuring that fans enjoy a rich and festive in-stadium experience, while making their safety and security paramount. At Super Bowl XLVIII, MetLife Stadium hosted 82,529 fans, in addition to approximately 10,000 vendors, staff, and members of the National and international media. Additionally, 112 million people watched the game on television. And in the week leading up to the game, tens of thousands of people attended official Super Bowl events at several locations in New Jersey and New York. Ensuring the safe and successful outcome of such a huge undertaking requires significant advance preparation and cooperation between a number of stakeholders, including State and Federal agencies as well as other public and private interests.

Over the past few decades, starting even before September 11, the NFL has developed extensive experience in applying protocols to facilitate cooperation and preparation among stakeholders responsible for designing and implementing Super Bowl security. These protocols have been continually refined over time. The NFL does not create the security plans for Super Bowls; that is the role of law enforcement and other public safety organizations. Instead, the NFL is a resource for these organizations, focusing on helping them with coordination and offering them its insights based on experience. Each Super Bowl is a unique event, depending on the characteristics of the location, the jurisdictions involved, and a number of other factors. One size does not fit all when it comes to planning Super Bowl security. The NFL's processes take these different needs into account by helping the coordination between State and Federal agencies who can apply their expertise to the circumstances of that particular Super Bowl. The following is a brief summary of our experiences in coordinating the preparation and implementation of a Super Bowl security plan.

IMPORTANCE OF ADVANCE PLANNING

The NFL normally begins planning for Super Bowl security about a year before the game by meeting with public safety officials and discussing broad plans. For Super Bowl XLVIII, we started with planning meetings about 2 years in advance of the game, based on the request of the New Jersey State Police, who along with the N.Y.P.D., were the lead public safety organization for the event. Our first meetings are generally with the Super Bowl's lead coordination and planning organization, which since Super Bowl XXXVI (the 2002 Super Bowl in New Orleans) have been State or local law enforcement agencies. That Super Bowl was designated a full National Special Security Event (NSSE), with the U.S. Secret Service as the main planning and coordinating public agency. Subsequent Super Bowls have been Special Event Assessment Rating (SEAR) 1 events, in which the lead planning and coordinating agency is a State or local one.

At these early meetings, we work on the basics of the security plans, for instance, determining which organization is responsible for which aspects of Super Bowl security. As the meetings continue, we focus on coordinating the efforts of the different organizations to ensure that their plans and protocols complement each other. These plans change as they are fine-tuned by the organizations, and we have found that in-person meetings are the best way to share information and keep the stakeholders updated throughout the planning process. We hold a planning meeting in April, a full production meeting in June, another planning meeting in October, and a final full production meeting in December. During the time leading up to the game, the group runs countless simulations of possible security events.

In addition, other security planners and I will generally attend five or six regular season games at the host stadium. These visits give us a first-hand look at the stadium in use and occupied by fans. Again, each Super Bowl is a unique event, depending on a variety of factors, some of which can be discovered only by experience. It is very important that the plan takes the different circumstances of Super Bowls into account. Super Bowl XLVIII was a cold-weather Super Bowl, held at an outdoor stadium. This factor affected our plan in a number of ways. For instance, we expected that fans would come to the game wearing winter coats and hats, therefore adding to the screening time that we normally see at warm weather Super Bowls. Although the cold weather turned out not to be an issue, seemingly minor details like fans' seasonal clothing need to be factored into the security plan.

NEED FOR COORDINATION

The coordination I have been describing is particularly important given the number of organizations involved and their varying roles. As I mentioned earlier, the identities of the lead security coordinating organizations depends on the security rating that the Department of Homeland Security gives to the event. When the Super Bowl is deemed an NSSE, like the 2002 New Orleans Super Bowl, the Secret Service is the lead security coordinating organization, and under other ratings, the lead organization is generally a State or local law enforcement agency for the jurisdiction in which the host stadium sits. The lead planning organization or organizations also depend on the circumstances of the particular Super Bowl. For Super Bowl XLVIII, although the game was held at MetLife Stadium in New Jersey, a number of significant events, such as the almost week-long Super Bowl Boulevard event, were held in New York City, so the New Jersey State Police and the N.Y.P.D. shared the responsibilities as co-leads. Public safety organizations from surrounding jurisdictions assisted with game-day security. When the game is being held in a jurisdiction with a smaller law enforcement agency, the coordination lead will generally consist of a coalition of local law enforcement agencies from surrounding jurisdictions and the State law enforcement. This is the case for Super Bowl 50, the 2016 Super Bowl, which will be held at Levi's Stadium, the San Francisco 49ers's home stadium, located in Santa Clara, California. The Santa Clara Police Department will be the lead agency, and it will receive significant support from other public safety organizations from surrounding jurisdictions.

A number of Federal agencies also play an integral role in preparing and implementing the security plan. The Federal Bureau of Investigation (FBI), Department of Homeland Security (DHS), and Secret Service are significant resources for the NFL and our public safety partners. They provide valuable intelligence, and lend their expertise in security planning. The FBI also works with State and local law enforcement and other Federal agencies to run background checks on the staff who will be working the Super Bowl. Customs and Border Protection (CBP) is also involved in the security plan and are responsible for searching and screening vehicles that come within the Super Bowl's secure perimeter. The U.S. Postal Service (USPS) is responsible for screening mail and parcels. Visible Intermodal Prevention and Response (VIPR) teams from the Transportation Security Administration (TSA) assist our State and local partners with mass transit security. The Federal Aviation Administration (FAA) is in charge of planning the Temporary Flight Restrictions (TFR) for the event, which restricts aircraft from flying in close proximity to the Super Bowl, and the U.S. Air Force and CBP enforce that perimeter. And for Super Bowl XLVIII, the Coast Guard provided security on the waterways surrounding MetLife Stadium.

There are also private contractors that the NFL uses for preparing and implementing the security plan. For instance, the NFL has worked with Populous, formerly known as HOK Sport, on security architecture for Super Bowl stadiums for at least 20 years. They assist in adapting the security plan to suit the stadium's physical structure and help determine where to put security structures, such as magnetometers and where to station certain security personnel.

GAME DAY

Our goal with all of the advance planning is to ensure that everything goes as planned, while at the same time preparing for any eventuality. It is absolutely vital that every organization knows its role and responsibilities and that information is shared among the organizations seamlessly and in real time. To help facilitate this cooperation and communication, senior officials from all of the stakeholders remain in a command post during the event. Decisions there can be made immediately, which is particularly important given the fluid nature of the plans and circumstances.

One of our biggest concerns is securing the stadium perimeter. Starting about a week before the game, the CBP, Department of Energy, and other Federal and State and local agencies work together to screen every vehicle that comes into the stadium secure perimeter. The TFR also protects the stadium perimeter by air, which is an extremely important component of Super Bowl security. For Super Bowl XLVIII game day, the FAA issued two TFRs. The first TFR, beginning at noon, was for a 1-nautical-mile ring around MetLife Stadium. No flights other than law enforcement flights were allowed within this 1-nautical-mile ring. The second TFR began at 5 p.m. It consisted of two rings, one with an 8-nautical-mile radius and one with a 30-nautical-mile radius. Only law enforcement flights were allowed within the 8-nautical-mile ring. Only aircraft squawking a transponder code and in contact with Air Traffic Control were allowed within the 30-nautical-mile radius ring. The CBP, and if necessary the Air Force, were responsible for enforcing the TFR. TFRs are very important for helping to ensure the security for all NFL games, and the Super Bowl in particular.

We are also have an extensive credential system in place to ensure that staff are where they are supposed to be. Perhaps unsurprisingly, many people want to be as near the field as possible. But we work closely with our Federal and State law enforcement partners to ensure that the credentials for sensitive areas are very tightly controlled and that on game day only properly credentialed individuals are in these locations. We use electronically restricted access and color-coded credentialing, and we train all staff to challenge anybody who does not have the proper credential for a given area.

CONCLUSION

Of course, this is just a brief summary of the massive undertaking that is securing the Super Bowl. Success requires the cooperation of and coordination with numerous organizations and countless people. The NFL is very thankful for the assistance of our Federal, State, and local partners, and we hope that we can continue to be a resource to them. Thank you again for the opportunity to testify today on such an important issue to the NFL and the Nation. I look forward to your questions.

Mrs. BROOKS. Thank you so much for your testimony, Mr. Grossi.

The Chairwoman now recognizes Mr. DeLorenzi to testify for 5 minutes.

STATEMENT OF DANIEL DE LORENZI, DIRECTOR, SECURITY AND SAFETY SERVICES, METLIFE STADIUM

Mr. DELORENZI. Good morning. First I would like to describe my role at MetLife Stadium. I represent the private sector. You know, we talk about the private sector here, and we have heard from public safety officials and how the——

Mrs. BROOKS. Could you speak a little closer to the mic?

Mr. DELORENZI. I'm sorry.

Mrs. BROOKS. Thank you. Is it on? Yes.

Mr. DELORENZI. I am going to describe my role as representing the private sector, specifically as it relates to the Super Bowl, but also in day-to-day operations. I can give you feedback. I know there is strong encouragement on a National level for public safety and the private sector to interact seamlessly, and I can assure you that takes place at MetLife Stadium, not only for the Super Bowl but for every event that we have there.

It is my job as the director of security not only—and we didn't talk about this very much. We talked about fire, police, law enforcement, but emergency medical service as well, another very important component of being able to prepare and respond to emergencies that may happen at the stadium.

I spend most of my time at the stadium making sure that everyone understands their role and how we are going to respond as a team, and that happens. In fact, in our command center on a day-to-day basis, for any event that we have at MetLife Stadium, we have representatives sitting side-by-side in our command center. You have an EMT person, a fire person, a police person, the FBI, and they sit there and they have face-to-face communications. It is the best way to operate. It works, and it encourages cooperation.

The two points I would like to make are I guess there is another group here that we didn't represent, and that is the civilian population, the security guards, the hundreds—I can't give you specific numbers, but close to a thousand people that we have working every event who are really not security guards. I talk to them and it is my job to train them and encourage them and motivate them and lead them to do this job, and it is a homeland security job that they are doing many times. The whole "see something, say something" is an important part of what they do.

We actually have guards out there—remember, they are screening not only vehicles but they are screening people, and we all know what they are screening for. They are there for a part-time job, but they are also there because they believe in what they are doing. If you don't believe in what you are doing, you are only there for a short time. I can say we have a very low turnover rate. These people come. They came after Super Storm Sandy last year for the New York Giants and the Pittsburgh Steelers game, when New Jersey was devastated in many areas, and these people show up week after week, and they do a great job. They work very closely with the police and fire and EMS.

But again, from a homeland security perspective, we know what the threats are. We don't have a generalized anxiety about what we are worrying about. We know specifically that we are worried about vehicle-borne threats, person-borne threats, those types of things, and we identify those things, and we do specific things not only with the civilian force but also with the sworn force of the police and the FBI.

So we are concentrating on the intelligence we have. We do a threat assessment and a vulnerability assessment every year for the stadium and for each event, not only the Super Bowl, for each game, which I like to think are National events when you have the Cowboys playing the Giants on Sunday Night Football and we have the Jets playing the Patriots on Monday Night Football. There is no doubt about it, that is a National event.

The Super Bowl came along. We did a lot of things. But I will tell you what, we do a lot of things for every single football game that you probably don't realize. I have the personal opinion that a lot of these things I do is because, yes, I was a public safety official before, but I am personally motivated to make sure that we leave nothing out of what we can reasonably be doing. I can assure you that we are doing everything we can possibly do. Thank you.

[The prepared statement of Mr. DeLorenzi follows:]

PREPARED STATEMENT OF DANIEL DELORENZI

The MetLife Stadium Emergency Management Plan provides guidance for emergency management policies and responsibilities in the event of an emergency or wide-spread disaster. MetLife Stadium has developed its Emergency Management Plan pursuant to the National Football League Best Practices for Security, the National Incident Management System, and the Incident Command System. The Incident Command System provides a standardized organizational structure to manage all types of emergencies and is designed to enable effective and efficient incident management that is used by all levels of government as well as private-sector organizations. The purpose of this plan is to organize MetLife Stadium operations and to support public safety counterparts to prepare for, respond to, and recover from a broad spectrum of emergencies, from small to complex incidents, both natural and man-made. MetLife Stadium has established an Incident Command structure that is designed to appropriately correspond with the Incident Command structure that will be employed by the various public safety agencies. Developing an emergency management plan to cover every conceivable disaster situation and response activity is impracticable. However, the concepts and components outlined in the MetLife Stadium plan have a broad range of applicability to a wide variety of emergencies that may occur. This plan provides guidance to allow MetLife Stadium to manage its responsibilities before, during, and after an emergency and can help meet the demand of a particular event or an escalating crisis. This is accomplished through a combination of training, planning, and coordination of resources and public safety resources.

Mrs. BROOKS. Thank you, Mr. DeLorenzi.

The Chairwoman now recognizes Mr. Boles to testify for 5 minutes.

STATEMENT OF J. DOUGLAS BOLES, PRESIDENT, INDIANAPOLIS MOTOR SPEEDWAY

Mr. BOLES. Thank you, Chairwoman Brooks, Ranking Member Payne, Congressman Pascrell. I am excited to be here on behalf of the Indianapolis Motor Speedway and the Hulman George Speedway and Hulman & Company, which is our parent company which owns the Indianapolis Motor Speedway.

I sat here this morning and listened to the first panel. I can't help but be struck by how much talk there was about the Super Bowl. We hosted the 46th Super Bowl in Indianapolis in 2012, and many of these conversations have taken place in our community. We would certainly like to host another Super Bowl.

What is unique about the Indianapolis Motor Speedway, our host committee chair for the 46th Super Bowl was Mark Miles, who is now the CEO of Hulman & Company, so my boss. So we often are talking about how do we work together with public safety agencies to make our event safe, as well as working with events that come into Indianapolis and how do we leverage the Indianapolis Motor Speedway to make those better?

The Indianapolis Motor Speedway is best known for the Indianapolis 500, an event that has been taking place since 1911. We just had our 98th Indianapolis 500 a little over 3 weeks ago, and we will host our 100th in 2016. I am not a mathematician myself, but knowing 1911 to 2016, it is hard to get to 100 when you put those together. We did skip a couple of events during World War I and World War II, and in 1945, after World War II, the Hulman George family actually bought the Indianapolis Motor Speedway and has continued to own it since then.

We are one of only three major race tracks in the United States that is not owned by a publicly-held corporation, and it is something that the family takes an awful lot of pride in, owning that organization and being part of Indianapolis.

With respect to our mass gathering planning and how we work with public service agencies, including emergency medical facilities and emergency medical companies who are helping us, we begin that essentially as soon as the race is over. So we have already started planning for 2015.

To give you a little bit of an idea about our facility itself, the facility is a 2½-mile race track built in 1909 that sits on 275 acres inside a 1,000-acre complex that we have. It seats a little over 240,000 people inside permanent seating. Those seats alone take up 20 acres. You could literally fit 15 Lucas Oil Fields inside of our Indianapolis Motor Speedway. So 15 of the stadiums that hosted the 46th Super Bowl can fit inside the Indianapolis Motor Speedway.

On race day, between public safety agency personnel, as well as our own personnel that are there, you have over 3,000 people working to make sure that they are taking care of the folks that come to the Indianapolis Motor Speedway each year as part of their Memorial Day traditions.

You know, I was also thinking a little bit about one of the things that makes us relatively unique is our customers. Those folks that buy tickets to the Indianapolis Motor Speedway come from all 50 States in the United States of America. They come from dozens of countries around the world. In fact, they bring media and drivers and fans of those drivers. We have several countries, including Venezuela, Russia, New Zealand, England, Australia, Japan, where our drivers come from to compete in the Indianapolis 500. It is truly a uniquely American event, but it fits very, very well inside a global motor sports scale, and it is the race of the year for most people with respect to motor sport.

In addition to the Indianapolis 500, we host three other events. We host a Nascar event that takes place at the end of July, and we host an international motorcycle event that takes place in August. That event is an event that is owned by a Spanish company. They bring in folks from all over the world. We probably have more international travelers for that event than we do for the Indianapolis 500. So we aren't just worried about our mass gathering safety and security and planning for the Indianapolis 500 but for our other events.

But to give you an idea of what the month of May looks like for those of us in Indianapolis, we kick the month of May off with the world's largest half-marathon that starts in downtown Indianapolis, roughly 40,000 runners. They actually run around the Indianapolis Motor Speedway and conclude back downtown in Indianapolis.

The following week we host the Grand Prix of Indianapolis, which is the Indy cars racing on the road course that we have at the Indianapolis Motor Speedway. Somewhere around 50,000 to 60,000 people attend that event.

Then we go into practice for the Indianapolis 500, and leading into the Indianapolis 500 race we actually have a big practice and concert that hosts nearly 75,000 people on Friday. We have a parade in downtown Indianapolis that hosts about 300,000 people lining the streets of Indianapolis. Then we have what the media report as over 300,000 people that attend the Indianapolis 500 when you take into consideration the folks that are actually inside the facility.

So it is a big, big event, not just in our community but globally.

Something that is probably of interest to this group is this year was the first year that we have gone from a SEAR 3 rating to a SEAR 2 rating. So it gave us an opportunity to really take what we practice with respect to our local, State, and other officials and how we integrate with the Federal Government as it related to the SEAR 2 rating.

We had a great experience this year. We started a little bit late. We are really looking forward to 2015 and already planning. But we were able to take advantage of some additional assets that made the event better for us with respect to some video camera surveillance opportunities, some helicopter opportunities. We had eight Homeland Security folks from Chicago that actually came down and helped us run our event.

It turned out to be a seamless relationship. I was just mentioning a moment ago that our concern there was not the support that we were going to get, but we have this group of 30-plus agencies that have worked together for several years to make the Indianapolis 500 what it was. We were concerned about adding in this new dynamic and how that was going to impact our ability to work together.

We found it to be very pleasant. It worked out very well. Actually, I think you could talk to all of our law enforcement officials and really believe that this involvement of the Federal Government was very beneficial. As I said, we are looking forward to 2015 and how that is going to play out, given more time to look at the resources to be prepared for the Indianapolis 500 as we lead into 2015.

With that said, I think what I will try to do is stay in touch with the committee and with Congresswoman Brooks. We will let you know how things are going with respect to 2015, how we can work together better. I think we will have more information for you with respect to how the Federal Government can work with what is a regional event on a huge, global scale, and we will hopefully be able to report back some good information there.

[The prepared statement of Mr. Boles follows:]

PREPARED STATEMENT OF J. DOUGLAS BOLES

JUNE 23, 2014

Chairwoman Brooks, Ranking Member McCaul, and Members of the subcommittee. I am pleased to appear before you today to discuss planning and preparation efforts for the largest single-day sporting event in the world, the Indianapolis 500, held annually at the Racing Capital of the World, the Indianapolis Motor Speedway in Speedway, Indiana.

We are proud to report that Hulman & Company, the parent company of the Indianapolis Motor Speedway (IMS) and the Verizon INDYCAR Series, recently concluded a successful month of May in Indianapolis, culminating with the crowning of Ryan Hunter-Reay as the champion of the 98th Running of the Indianapolis 500.

Annually, the Indianapolis Motor Speedway hosts four major automotive racing events. The most famous is the Indianapolis 500, which is the signature event of what we refer to as our "Month of May." Our month features the country's largest participation half-marathon, the OneAmerica 500 Festival Mini-Marathon; the Verizon INDYCAR Grand Prix of Indianapolis; two consecutive days of Indianapolis 500 qualifications; two major concerts that attract upwards of 50,000 people each; the IPL 500 Festival Parade, and the Indianapolis 500-Mile Race.

Our planning and preparation is year-round and never rests, and our top priority is the safety and security of everyone who is in and around our facility. We have the highest expectations for ourselves and our local public safety agencies as we collectively prepare to host hundreds of thousands of guests each year. Our fans are passionate about our facility and our races, and our employees and partners are even more passionate about protecting our most valuable assets, those legions of fans that make a visit to the Indianapolis Motor Speedway in May an annual tradition.

A look at our facility and some history will provide some perspective.

The Indianapolis Motor Speedway was constructed in 1909, a 2.5-mile track that inhabits 275 acres of land inside our 1,000-acre campus. IMS has nearly 240,000 permanent seats covering approximately 20 acres. Four holes of our renowned 18-hole championship golf course, the Brickyard Crossing, are contained within the track oval, as is our museum, interior named streets, the iconic Pagoda, nearly 200 luxury suites, other hospitality areas, garages, and an on-site level 1-rated trauma medical facility (the busiest emergency room in the State of Indiana on the day of the Indianapolis 500).

Together, Yankee Stadium, the Rose Bowl, Churchill Downs, the Roman Colosseum, and Vatican City all can fit inside the IMS oval—at the same time.

The first racing surface at IMS was crushed rock and tar, not ideal for the inaugural automobile race in August 1909 for which 65 cars were entered. That fall, track owners, led by Carl Fisher, decided to accept the recommendation of a National paving brick organization and resurface the track with street-paving bricks. Over 63 days, 3.2 million bricks—each weighing 9½ pounds, were laid on the oval surface, and the term "The Brickyard" was coined. Many of those bricks remain today under several layers of asphalt. Some portion of the bricks were maintained as a part of the racing surface until 1961, and even today, competitors take the checkered flag at the The Yard of Bricks.

Following the first racing on the bricks in 1910, organizers settled on a 500-mile format over Memorial Day weekend and the Indianapolis 500 was born. Ray Harroun took the checkered flag in 1911 in 6 hours and 42 minutes, driving an average speed of 74.602 miles per hour. By comparison, in 2013, Tony Kanaan won the Indianapolis 500 with an average speed of 187.433 miles per hour. Qualifying speeds regularly exceed 230 mph.

The race continued until World War I forced cancellation in 1917 and 1918, but it resumed again in 1919 and took off in popularity, and continued until World War II when motor racing was again brought to a halt. From 1942 to 1945 the track fell into disrepair and some thought that at the conclusion of the war, the facility would be sold to developers and divided for post-war housing.

Following the War, Terre Haute, Indiana businessman Anton "Tony" Hulman, Jr., purchased the race track in 1945 and a massive undertaking began to get the track back in shape. Mr. Hulman embarked on a renovation project that brought the facility back to life, and it re-opened for the 1946 Indianapolis 500.

Today, IMS remains owned and operated by Hulman-George Family and is one of only three tracks in the United States outside the operation of Speedway Motorsports, Inc., or International Speedway Corporation. The Hulman-George Family continues to lead efforts to grow the sport of open wheel racing and is setting the stage for the second 100 years of racing at the Indianapolis Motor Speedway as the 100th running of the Indianapolis 500 approaches in 2016.

IMS and the Indianapolis 500 have hosted many celebrities and dignitaries over the years, including Presidents Gerald Ford, Ronald Reagan, George H.W. Bush, and Bill Clinton, Chief Justice John Roberts, cabinet secretaries, and foreign ambassadors.

IMS is set to embark on a nearly $100 million upgrade project that will introduce cutting-edge technology, infrastructure upgrades, and fan experience engagement. The last major construction project at IMS occurred from 1998–2000 when the current Pagoda control tower and its adjacent plaza, pit-side garages and road course were built. The latest addition to our campus will be unveiled next week when we cut the ribbon on a 25-acre solar farm on our property, the largest such system hosted at a sporting facility.

IMS is located in the small town of Speedway, Indiana, which is enveloped by the city of Indianapolis. Downtown Indianapolis is located a mere 5 miles from the Speedway and the track is surrounded by neighborhoods, major traffic thoroughfares and industry, such as our neighbors Praxair and Allison Transmission.

As the president of the Indianapolis Motor Speedway, I am responsible for all of our preparations to host on-site major sporting events each year. Our challenges are many; however, it would be impossible for us to provide a safe and secure environment for our fans without the public safety partners and agencies that help us coordinate security, crowd management, and traffic control and provide us with valuable intelligence.

Although the race itself is usually run from start to finish in about 3 hours on the Sunday of Memorial Day Weekend, race day has begun long before the cannon sounds at 5:30 a.m. to mark the official opening of the track to spectators. The track opening begins a morning of pageantry that includes marching bands, recognition of all branches of the United States military, celebration of the rich history of IMS, the singing of *America the Beautiful, God Bless America* and *Back Home Again in Indiana,* and the famous command to drivers to "start your engines," given by family matriarch Mari Hulman George.

IMS counts on the expertise and manpower of the Town of Speedway Police and Fire Departments. Speedway Police Chief Jim Campbell and Speedway Fire Chief Mark Watson both have a wealth of knowledge about our facility and understand our unique needs.

Our list of partners is long, but each is an important component of our public safety plan:
- Town of Speedway Police and Fire Departments
- Indianapolis Metropolitan Police Department
- Marion County Sheriff's Office
- Indiana State Police
- Indiana State Excise Police
- Indiana National Guard
- Indiana University Health
- Federal Bureau of Investigation
- United States Secret Service
- Transportation Security Administration
- Federal Aviation Administration
- U.S. Department of Homeland Security
- National Weather Service

During May, IMS depends heavily on the support of public safety agencies, all leading to the Indianapolis 500 race day, when 800 public safety personnel are on site by 6 a.m. In addition, IMS employs more than 1,600 people responsible for parking operations, ticket/gate entrance, guest services, grandstands, spectator mounds, and subcontracted security.

For the first time in 2014, the Indianapolis 500 was designated as a Special Event Assessment Rating II. The SEAR rating previously was III but was changed following the scrutiny of large events after the 2013 Boston Marathon tragedy.

In this initial year of SEAR II rating, we became more acquainted with resources that are now available to us to assist with the ingress and egress of hundreds of thousands of people in a 12-hour period. This year, IMS was assigned a Federal agent from the U.S. Department of Homeland Security, who provided us with important real-time feedback, additional security cameras, and the use of two helicopters for traffic control as well as aerial security coverage.

Now that we are developing relationships with the Federal SEAR II team, we will be better-prepared with additional expertise and more knowledge in the years ahead.

On race day, we operate from four command centers: Our primary center in the track infield, two outside and one on stand-by as a back-up. We use a Unified Command system associated with the National Incident Management System in each of the centers.

A formal chain of command is established and known to all. For IMS, the center is manned by the senior director of operations, director of engineering and construction, and representatives of security, traffic, gates, parking, garages and pits, stands and mounds, guest services, medical, and weather. The police command includes representatives from local and State police agencies.

IMS also has a sophisticated and extensive public address system, which is attached to multiple large screen video displays located throughout the facility. The system not only provides audio and video race information but has the ability to communicate any emergency notifications. The public address booth and video control room are located in the primary command center. This gives the unified command the ability to provide up-to-the-minute information about any situation warranted.

IMS was one of the first venues in the country to implement the Department of Homeland Security's "See Something, Say Something" campaign including a visit from Secretary Janet Napolitano to kick off the program in 2011. Posters are located throughout IMS and two INDYCAR drivers recorded a video campaign that aired on-site during the month of May. We credit the program for an increase in the number of reports of suspicious activities and packages we receive from fans.

In 2015, IMS will add a new texting system to improve real-time interaction with our customers. The system will allow fans to text questions, comments, or emergency information to the command center, and IMS will react and respond accordingly.

Our primary command center is operational 24 hours a day, 7 days a week beginning a week before the official opening of the Indianapolis Motor Speedway in May and closes several days after the Indianapolis 500. We operate the same system for our other major racing events.

Our planning for security and related matters is year-round. Monthly meetings to plan for 2015 have already begun with representatives from public safety agencies and will continue throughout the year. As a part of our year-round planning, staff is in regular contact by phone, email, and texts with several members of public safety agencies to maintain the dialogue about our events and other events taking place in central Indiana.

By March of each year, our planning sessions become devoted to specific topics, including executive protection, intelligence, gang control, crowd management, and parking. In April, we conduct a table-top security exercise and begin on-site training to expose public safety officials and track personnel not only to the sheer physical size of IMS but to handle specific situations.

Emergency preparedness involves many scenarios, including in-venue non-terrorist events, such as a grandstand collapse or fire, as well as preparation for a terrorist threat and, of course, training to deal with on-track incidents.

When the calendar reaches May, staff and partners at IMS are in full event mode. There are regular and unscheduled updates from Federal officials when information and intelligence warrants. Daily operational meetings with and without law enforcement are conducted and daily operations movements are outlined to orchestrate the daily schedule of activities.

Following each major event, IMS meets with its public safety partners to complete an after-action report that includes written reports about opportunities for improvement for future events. The operations team at IMS uses the report to make future planning decisions.

Over decades of hosting successful race events, we've learned that building and maintaining relationships on all levels is a key to success. We ask a lot of our public safety partners—sometimes too much of them. We also try to be a good partner by providing meeting space and access to train on our grounds to help meet our needs.

Public safety officials at local, State, and Federal levels know, understand, and buy in to the Indianapolis Motor Speedway and its importance to the city, the State of Indiana, and racing fans from around the world. Only with them can we continue to host The Greatest Spectacle in Racing.

We look forward to working with this committee to assist in any way we can with information that is helpful in local and Federal coordination of large-scale events.

Mrs. BROOKS. Thank you, Mr. Boles.

The Chairwoman now recognizes Dr. Roberts to testify for 5 minutes. Thank you.

STATEMENT OF FRED S. ROBERTS, DIRECTOR, DEPARTMENT OF HOMELAND SECURITY CENTER OF EXCELLENCE, COMMAND CONTROL AND INTEROPERABILITY CENTER FOR ADVANCED DATA ANALYSIS, RUTGERS UNIVERSITY

Mr. ROBERTS. So, thank you, Congresswoman Brooks and Congressman Payne and Congressman Pascrell, for your leadership not only on this topic but also on all aspects of homeland security.

It is an honor for me to be invited to testify before this committee. As Mr. Payne noted, I am a professor, a professor of mathematics, in fact, at Rutgers University. I direct the Command, Control, and Interoperability Center for Advanced Data Analysis. That is a mouthful. We call it CCICADA in short. CCICADA was founded as a Department of Homeland Security University Center of Excellence.

So we are based at Rutgers, but like the rest of the university centers, we are a network. So we have partners all around the country, and, in particular, as Congresswoman Brooks has mentioned, we are delighted to partner with our sister center at Purdue. They deal with visual analytics. They have done some remarkable work on visualizing data and gaining understanding from visualization.

So, we work on modeling, we work on simulation, we work on helping make decisions, and we work on all aspects of homeland security that are data-related. So I would like to take a moment to say that DHS has been a strong supporter of our work on stadium security, and it is only really through DHS support that we have developed real expertise in this area.

We are still learning, and many of the people that you have heard from are the kinds of people we have learned from. We certainly could never have developed the skill and expertise that we have without the support of DHS Office of University Programs.

So our work on stadiums commenced in 2010 when we worked on simulation of how to evacuate a stadium. We worked on that in part with the private sector, with our partner Regal Decision Systems. The evacuation tool that was developed actually was implemented when MetLife was opened, very shortly thereafter, with an evacuation required because of a lightning storm. It turned out that the evacuation planning and model actually helped with that evacuation.

So we have now, because of our work on stadium security, interacted with all major sports leagues, as well as college and minor sports leagues, minor leagues, and I will come back to that observation. We have also studied safety at other large gathering places—malls, bus terminals, amusement parks, and so on. So certainly those places are attractive targets for criminals and terrorists, and increasingly more so as targets such as the Pentagon or the U.S. Capitol are hardened.

We began to collaborate with stadiums on patron screening, and we eventually developed a tool that enables the stadiums to determine which types of inspection might work best in their environment, taking into account how many patrons you expect, the type of event, the weather conditions, amount of time each inspection process takes. Because of the success of that tool, I as an academic was actually out in California last week to give a presentation to the NFL's meeting of stadiums and venues security directors.

We have also worked on crowd management and prevention of human trafficking, starting with the Indianapolis Super Bowl.

I have also had the opportunity to work with the DHS Office of SAFETY Act Implementation. We were asked to develop a best practices manual for stadium security that would both be useful to the Office as a tool to evaluate applications from stadiums for SAFETY Act designation or certification, but also to use as a tool in preparing applications if you were a stadium or a venue. So as part of the process of developing that manual, we did an extensive literature search, we visited venues, held interviews, and actually had a nice workshop at Rutgers Stadium in 2013 on this topic.

So we are now working with the Office to develop new measures of effectiveness and ways of testing the effectiveness of security plans, and they have asked us to work on economics of stadium security as well as randomization techniques to look at screening and credentialing.

So I just wanted to mention a few examples to the extent I have time of the things we have observed that were a little bit of a surprise both to us and to the security folks we have talked to.

We have talked already about cyber here. Everybody knows that cyber is an important issue. What a lot of people don't understand is that today's modern automobile is a collection of physical systems that are run by computers, and they are becoming semi-autonomous already, and it may be that one day soon we will have driverless cars.

We already know how to hack into a car and control its braking and steering and acceleration, and one of my scenarios that I worry about is somebody doing that in the parking lot of a major event.

Magnetometers, walk-through magnetometers, another major issue. The stadiums are very interested in and the NFL has asked the stadiums to look into the implementation of walk-throughs. There are a lot of interesting issues there, including how well they will work outside in bad weather, issues as to whether you should put them on wheels and put them out of the way in case you have an evacuation problem, issues as to how much they cost and how many you need, and how many stadiums can afford them, and should a stadium in fact get some incentive or management get some incentive for implementing the latest and the best security devices.

Food security is an issue that not many people are very aware of. Something as simple as not putting out mustard and ketchup in these big dispensers, which could easily be tampered with, and putting out little condiment packages is just one little piece of food security that we have learned about.

Information about the physical facilities at a stadium is often part of the public record after a new stadium is built is that of vulnerability we have to worry about.

Background checks for employees, we have heard about that. We do credential checking for stadium employees, but repeat background checks are not done so regularly. They are expensive. Again, there is the issue of how you get them done. But are there possibly randomization techniques that might allow us to do this occasionally for some of the employees?

Emergency plans, are they given to all the employees? If so, when they leave the employ, do they go with them? Is there control over them?

So as I said, I work in all kinds of venues. Some of them are very impressive. The big ones have gotten SAFETY Act certification or designation. That, then, leads you to look at venues that are not as well off as the Yankees and MetLife folks and so on.

So just as the Capitol and the Pentagon have been hardened, and that has led us to the major stadiums, the major stadiums, as they get hardened, lead us to look at minor leagues. That, I think, is an issue where, if something happens at a minor league stadium, it is going to have a major impact on the United States and on the major sports leagues. So it is an area where we need to be aware.

Finally, let me talk about the Boston Marathon. We have had that mentioned. The difficulty of protecting crowds that gather for events where there is no natural access control point is a serious issue. We have looked—this past week New Jersey was honored to host the USA Special Olympics, the third Special Olympics we have had in this country. We had our students out observing.

It is hard to control access at Mercer County Park where the soccer and the tennis and the softball were played, very much similar to the kinds of problems we faced with the Boston Marathon. We will be working on the after-action report with the Special Olympics. We had discussion about how you get it to the next group that is going to be running an event of this sort. Lots of difficult issues that emanate from such events, and this was not a done deal.

In closing, there are certainly a lot of opportunities for us to collaborate—private sector, academics, public sector. We in academics stand ready to hopefully play a role. So, thank you, and I will be happy to answer any questions.

[The prepared statement of Mr. Roberts follows:]

PREPARED STATEMENT OF FRED S. ROBERTS

JUNE 23, 2014

My name is Fred Roberts. I am a professor of mathematics at Rutgers University in Piscataway, NJ and I am director of the Command, Control, and Interoperability Center for Advanced Data Analysis (CCICADA). CCICADA was founded as a Department of Homeland Security University Center of Excellence, is based at Rutgers, and has 16 partner institutions across the United States. It is part of the network of Centers of Excellence created by the DHS Office of University Programs. CCICADA's work is based on data analysis and we work on modeling, simulation, and decision support. We work with many Federal, State, regional, and local government agencies and with the private sector.

DHS has been a strong supporter of CCICADA's work on stadium security. Through the DHS university programs support, we feel that we have developed a real expertise in this area, one we could never have developed without DHS University programs. This work commenced in 2010 when we worked on simulation of stadium evacuation in collaboration with one of our private-sector partners, Regal Decision Systems. Regal's evacuation tool helped half a dozen stadiums plan evacuations and was instrumental in allowing MetLife Stadium in New Jersey to evacuate safely during a preseason game in its first year of operation when there was a lightning storm.

Work on stadium evacuation has led us to collaborate with all major sports leagues, as well as college and minor league sports, and also to study safety and security at malls, bus and rail terminals, amusement parks, and other places where people gather. These gathering places are attractive targets for terrorists and criminals, and increasingly more so as such iconic targets as the Pentagon and the Capitol are "hardened."

Based on our early work on stadium evacuation, we began to collaborate with stadiums on patron screening procedures and eventually developed a tool that enables stadiums to determine which types of inspection (wanding, pat-downs, bag inspections, walk-through magnetometers) will work best in their environment, taking into account the number of patrons expected, the weather conditions, the amount of time each type of inspection takes, etc. Because of the initial success of this tool, I was asked to present it to the National Football League's security seminar last week, a meeting attended by security directors of stadiums and venues all across the NFL.

We have also worked on models of crowd management and on prevention of human trafficking at major sports events such as the Super Bowl.

In 2012, CCICADA was asked by the DHS Office of SAFETY Act Implementation to develop a "Best Practices Manual" for stadium security from a counter-terrorism point of view. This manual, delivered in July 2013, was meant for OSAI to use as a tool to evaluate applications from stadiums for SAFETY Act designation or certification, and for stadiums to use as a tool in preparing their applications. As part of the process of developing that manual, we did an extensive literature review and held interviews with and visited venues from all major sports leagues, as well as college and minor leagues. We also held a workshop on stadium security at Rutgers in 2013. We are now working on additional aspects of stadium security for OSAI, expanding on our earlier work, to develop metrics, measures of effectiveness, and good ways to test for training. OSAI would also like us to work on the economics of stadium security and on the use of randomization in screening, credentialing, and other aspects of stadium security.

Our work has led us to some observations that were a surprise not only to us but to a number of the security experts we interacted with. Here are a few examples.

Increasingly, physical systems are run by cyber systems. In our modern stadiums, this is true of heating and air conditioning, message boards (including for emergency messages), access control within the facility, escalators and elevators. But these systems can fail due to deliberate action of others. Thus, cybersecurity in our Nation's stadiums is a major concern. At Super Bowl XLVII in New Orleans, the lights suddenly went out. My first reaction was that this was a cyber attack. Fortunately I was wrong. However, it was a warning sign.

While a great deal of attention has been paid to hardening access to a stadium, the exterior of the stadium becomes a softer target. Today's modern automobile is a good example of a collection of physical systems that are increasingly run by cyber systems. Modern cars are already semi-autonomous and there is work being done on totally driverless cars. We have already seen that it is possible to hack into a modern car and control its braking, acceleration, steering, etc. What would happen if someone hacked into a car in the busy parking lot when thousands of people are packed together tailgating?

There is a great deal of consensus that walk-through magnetometers are more effective in detecting dangerous materials than other screening systems such as wanding or pat-down. Yet, there are issues that need to be resolved about magnetometers. Early evidence seems to be that they might not work so well in bad weather, especially wind. Also, so that they don't block the way in case of the need to evacuate, at least one stadium has experimented with putting them on wheels. But does this affect their accuracy? Magnetometers also involve a major capital expense for a venue and because they require much more space than wanding or pat-down, might even require a stadium to give up some of its parking lot to make room for them. What incentives are there for management to do this?

Food security is an issue addressed with widely varying degrees of effectiveness and thoroughness at our Nation's stadiums. Effective measures can be as simple as putting out condiments in packets, rather than large dispensers that make targets of opportunity for chemical or biological agents. However, not all stadiums are well-versed in food security.

Information about the physical facilities at a stadium is often available to the public, e.g., when new building plans are filed. This could be a serious vulnerability.

Background checks for employees are a key component of a stadium security plan. But it is very difficult to find out about changes in background after an employee has been hired. How does one find out about new problems with the law, for example? Could repeat of background checks be required? They are expensive, and one possible model might be to perform them randomly from time to time.

Domestic violence/workplace violence are issues for stadiums. Disgruntled spouses and others can be a problem. Does the stadium obtain information about restraining orders that employees are served? Should it be easier to obtain such information than it is now?

Do employees receive a copy of an emergency plan? Are they required to return it when they leave employment? Do they receive it electronically and, if so, how can we be sure they do not make and/or maintain a copy?

As I said, our work has taken us to all kinds of venues. Several, such as Yankee Stadium, MetLife Stadium, Citi Field, have already received SAFETY act designation or certification. Achieving such status reflects the professionalism and extensive emphasis on security at these venues. However, less well-off owners of venues and sports franchises do not have the resources to invest in security in the way that these large and highly successful examples do, and this is even more the case for minor league venues. Just as "hardening" of the Pentagon and U.S. Capitol and other iconic targets can direct the attention of terrorists to iconic sports stadiums, hardening of those stadiums can direct the attention of terrorists to sports venues that are less secure. If the object is to disrupt the enjoyment of our gathering places, and create terror, an attack at a minor league venue could have a significant impact.

The events at the Boston Marathon demonstrate the difficulty of protecting large crowds that gather for events where there is no natural access control. Last week our students and faculty were official security observers at the USA Special Olympics in New Jersey, where some of the venues had similar issues of access control, and we will be helping the Special Olympics management write an After-Action Report that will inform the next organizers of this important event. We have already learned from the Boston Marathon to take measures at our stadiums where access control is possible to set up perimeters so as to minimize the possibility that screening procedures themselves will create vulnerabilities by creating long lines of people in a small space. However, Boston-type vulnerabilities exist in the areas outside the stadium screening areas.

It is not possible to protect people in large gathering places from all hazards, especially in an open society such as ours. However, with appropriate research, with true partnerships among Government, the private sector, and even those of us in academics, the risk can hopefully be reduced.

Mrs. BROOKS. Thank you. As a true academic, you have caused us all to think about some things that maybe we hadn't completely thought about.

With that, I would like to turn it over to Congressman Pascrell, who can only be with us a short time longer.

Mr. PASCRELL. Thank you very much. I appreciate that.

Dr. Roberts, you brought up a lot of things that we hadn't gotten into today and are very critical. You are looking to the future, and I think that is very, very important.

Every day, every day our enemies probe our systems, every day, not every other day, every day. So we can't have a crisis-oriented strategy. This is every day of the year, and it is important to me and everybody on the panel, and it is important to you, I know. I thank you for your work.

I thank you all for coming here today.

This is a question I have. I was going to get into the cost of this, who picks up the cost, but I will follow up another avenue perhaps another time.

Dan, it is always good to see you. You do a great job at the Meadowlands. You have always done a good job.

Any of you—Mr. Grossi, Mr. DeLorenzi, Mr. Boles, Dr. Roberts— what do you think has to change in order for us to have a better coordinated or the best coordinated system for our large events, our mass events; and, as Dr. Roberts says, smaller events too? Because terrorists look for the least likely place, and we have to understand that.

Mr. Grossi.

Mr. GROSSI. I think the level of cooperation and the in-person meetings, just the simple human dynamics of getting to know everyone. That is what we do at the NFL. We start working year out. We don't come into the Super Bowl city in December and expect to get everything done in January and have the game in early February.

We come in, we establish relationships with law enforcement, with all the public safety groups, with the stadiums, and I think it is going forward the relationships that we build and nurture throughout the year that, when it comes time for the game on Super Bowl Sunday, everybody is ready and everybody is communicating and everybody knows exactly what their role is.

Mr. PASCRELL. Just one yes or no. Do you have the resources to do the job to protect the American people at the events pertaining to the National Football League? Do you have the resources?

Mr. GROSSI. Absolutely.

Mr. PASCRELL. Thank you.

Mr. GROSSI. Yes, sir.

Mr. PASCRELL. Dan, what would you change?

Mr. DELORENZI. I think it has changed already. I think in the old days, I will say the '80s, the '90s, prior to 9/11, as a police chief here in the city of Newark, there was a lot of siloed decision making with the Fire Department, the Police Department, and the EMS were left out a lot of times.

I think a lot of that has changed. In fact, probably most of it has changed, and that is good news, and I think the public should know that. Everyone has an equal voice. The Fire Department was at the Super Bowl, and it made me feel better knowing they were there. It makes me feel better knowing that EMS has a mass casualty plan. I think the Lieutenant Colonel said you step aside and you let them do what they are supposed to do.

The whole unified command structure, that is a standard decision-making process across the country, and everyone has bought into that too, where there is no one boss. Typically, the police were the boss in the old days. That has gone away. A smart police commander will know that if it is a fire decision, the fire commander will make the decision. If it is a medical decision, EMS. So that whole incident command system has taken hold. We use it for every event. We use it for the Super Bowl, and it works.

Again, that is part of the post-9/11 NIMS. The National system for coordination and decision making, I can assure you, has taken hold.

Mr. PASCRELL. Thank you.

Mr. Boles.

Mr. BOLES. Congresswoman Brooks and I had an opportunity to talk this morning, and I think this is kind-of important with respect to your question. We at the Indianapolis Motor Speedway own also the Verizon Indy Car Series which produces Indy Car races throughout the country, and we are able to go in and talk to some of our promoters inside different communities and help them to actually prepare to put on an event, but also with respect to working with their law enforcement agencies and how to prepare for those mass gathering events.

I think one of the things we probably don't do very well at is how do we take the learnings that we have as the Indianapolis Motor Speedway and the Verizon Indy Car Series and then begin to work with other folks like the NFL, like the NBA, like the NCAA. Being in Indianapolis, we have the benefit of hosting the Final Four, having hosted a Super Bowl. So there are a lot of resources there that we can take advantage of. But certainly Nationally, I am sure there are several things that took place during the 48th Super Bowl that we could learn as an organization to make the Indianapolis Motor Speedway and our events, as well as the Verizon Indy Car Series.

So I think it might be helpful to have a mechanism for us to communicate across sports, across mass gathering type of events, and maybe that is something that Dr. Roberts, who is beginning to gather that, is there a place we could learn. His testimony alone gives me great pause to start thinking about things we need to be prepared for.

So I think it is just maybe taking that communication that we all feel we are doing well at an incident level or at an event level, and then how do we learn from others so that we can raise the tide for all of us.

Mr. PASCRELL. Very good.

What do you think of that, Dr. Roberts?

Mr. ROBERTS. So I think, first of all, to step back, as a relative newcomer to this type of planning and preparation and so on, I have been amazed and impressed with what the stadium folks do. A lot of it comes from sharing information. So information sharing really is a key to this whole thing, I think, for us to learn from what others do and for us to improve what we do.

I would like in particular to mention what we do here in New Jersey. The New Jersey Office of Homeland Security and Preparedness, which is really a leader in stadium security and large gathering security, has quarterly sports and large gathering security meetings, and those are very impressive. They share information. They share best practices. They introduce the folks who maybe don't have the resources that the larger groups do to the things the larger groups are doing and so on.

That does lead to another idea which has come up in some of our discussions which is maybe a little bit off the wall, and that is sharing of equipment and sharing of software which runs with certain vulnerabilities, but it is something that we have talked about and whether that is a possibility.

Finally, I think the kind of thing that the Office of SAFETY Act Implementation has had us do, which is develop best practices manuals; and hopefully, eventually, when their lawyers get done with our manual, it will be given wide-spread circulation. I think that that is a key.

Mr. PASCRELL. Thank you very much.

Thanks to the panel.

Thank you, Madam Chairlady. I appreciate that.

Thank you, Donald, and good luck for the rest of the hearing.

I am sorry I have to leave.

Mrs. BROOKS. No, and thank you, Congressman Pascrell, for joining us. We very much appreciate it. We wish you were on our subcommittee. You are welcome to join us at any time at any of our hearings. Terrific questions and terrific support for our efforts. Thank you.

At this time, I will turn it over to my Ranking Member, Congressman Payne, for 5 minutes of questioning.

Mr. PAYNE. Thank you.

Mr. Grossi, as you observed in your testimony, each Super Bowl is unique. Can you talk about how you adapt security operations to address the needs and vulnerabilities in each host city?

Mr. GROSSI. Yes. As I said, our planning starts about a year out. Again, the configuration of stadiums, stadium locations, they are all different. As Colonel Cetnar alluded to earlier in his testimony, he talked about Indianapolis and New Orleans, which both Super Bowl sites were in a downtown area. At MetLife, we had the luxury of having a surrounding area, acres and acres of open area and parking lots which, quite frankly, makes it easier to secure. We put up a 300-foot hard perimeter, and we established our perimeter a week out.

In New Orleans and in Indianapolis, we didn't have that luxury of establishing the perimeter for a week because of major roads and thoroughfares which would have been an impact to traffic and to people coming in and out of New Orleans and Indianapolis. So we modified our plan. We had a partial lockdown throughout the week, and then Friday morning we went into the hard lockdown that we normally do on the previous Monday.

So we adapt for each stadium based on its location and the individual characteristics of that stadium.

Mr. PAYNE. Thank you.

To follow up, having adequate and timely information on security threats is critical to your ability to keep the players, performers, and spectators at a mass gathering safe. What can you tell us about DHS' responses with respect to your informational needs? How have you seen your feedback on intelligence products incorporated into the Department's private-sector information-sharing process?

Let's start with Mr. Boles.

Mr. BOLES. This year really was the first year we had an opportunity to work directly with DHS. We had a relationship with the FBI for several years, and we found that the communication from both organizations has been very good, flowing in both directions. So with respect to any potential threats or any conversation in and around our events, we have been able to have an open line of communication. We feel like that has been very helpful.

As I said, with respect to the DHS and the SEAR 2 level increase for us this year, that was very beneficial for us. One of the places that we really felt like we needed some help was in being able to monitor our external ingress and egress from the facility, monitor our perimeters, and we were able to secure some additional video cameras to help us monitor that. We, similar to MetLife Stadium, have a control command area where all of the agencies sit together, face each other, are able to talk. We have all the video boards where they can watch that. We also have two external command centers as well, so that there are three of them in operations. But the one main one allows our folks to talk. Department of Homeland Security was there, so we had up-to-the-minute information to the extent that we needed it in and around our event.

So I think as we go forward and we build that relationship, I think that is just going to get better for us, and it is just going to make it better for our participants and for our customers and those folks that visit the Speedway.

Mr. PAYNE. Thank you.

Mr. DeLorenzi.

Mr. DeLORENZI. One of the things I am proud to say, we have a great relationship with DHS Science and Technology. In fact, we spent the last 2 or 3 years participating in the SAFETY Act accreditation process, and in December we were fortunate enough to be the first NFL stadium that is SAFETY Act certified. A lot of people think SAFETY Act certified applies to a technology, and that was its original intent. But our application was basically a several-hundred-page application that came down to a thesis paper on how MetLife Stadium acts as a homeland security system, a multi-layered system starting with the parking lots and the people, the training, the technology, the procedures. All of that is wrapped up in this application.

It was important to me to have this accreditation from DHS. I saw it as a validation of everything that we are doing, and having someone from the caliber of the people they have in Science and Technology look at it and say, yes, you are doing a great job, you are SAFETY Act certified, and we were able to attain that.

Mr. PAYNE. Thank you.

Mr. Grossi.

Mr. GROSSI. Again, working with the stadiums, it is our goal—and to Danny's credit, he worked hard on the SAFETY Act accreditation, and that is our goal. Eventually, most NFL stadiums will be accredited under the SAFETY Act.

Mr. PAYNE. Okay, thank you.

Madam Chairwoman, I yield back.

Mrs. BROOKS. I now recognize myself for 5 minutes of questioning.

We haven't talked a huge amount about the concerns about cyber attacks. With so much of our world counting on technology and the cyber world, I would like to just ask the organizations how you prevent and protect against a cyber attack. Whether it is the Super Bowl or games or the Motor Speedway, it is something that we in Congress are very, very focused on, working with the private sector and the public sector. But it is of grave concern to us.

So, Mr. Boles, I might start with you.

Mr. BOLES. With respect to how we communicate to our fans in particular, we do rely heavily on text messaging. We rely heavily on the communication that the law enforcement agencies have with each other. We have basically a television production studio that sits just outside of the pagoda command where all of our law enforcement are gathered, and that is one of the best ways to communicate to our 300,000-plus fans inside the venue, through radio communications, through video board communications.

So from our standpoint, the cyber communication protection of that is important because that is how we will be able to deliver messages to our folks in the event that something happens. We have an IT department that is there all year that is beginning to pay attention to those. Cyber attacks with respect to events like ours are relatively new, and we are looking forward to information from folks like Dr. Roberts on how we can better prepare for those type of items.

With respect to our parking lots and cars and the technology of those things, those are certainly things that we will put on our radar screen to begin to understand. But especially as we lean towards technology as a way to communicate evacuation plans or weather information or things we believe are important to our folks in the seat, it is important that we are able to protect the integrity of those systems that deliver it, and we have full-time staff to do that, as well as consultants to help us try to understand that.

Mrs. BROOKS. Thank you.

Mr. DeLorenzi, I assume with getting a SAFETY Act designation—and congratulations for that—that certainly your protection against cyber attacks must be part of that.

Mr. DELORENZI. Yes.

Mrs. BROOKS. Can you share with us what you can?

Mr. DELORENZI. Yes. We had three different groups of experts come into the stadium and assess. You know, cybersecurity does come down to physical things that are in place, right? Firewalls and such. We had three different expert groups come in and do individual assessments of our different systems, and I think that is the best way to do it. You can sit there and talk about things and IT people—yes, I have that and I have this—but until they come in and actually see it and do a physical assessment and inspection, that is when they can get the assurance.

We had them done by the FBI. We had them done by the New Jersey State Police and DHS. I will say that there were a couple of things uncovered and fixed in all those instances.

We also get—and it just happened yesterday. The Rock put out something on malware, because there are always new things coming. There are always new viruses and malware that is out there. I get those emails as a security director. I immediately forward that to our chief technology officer and he gets it, and that has to happen. I just can't sit on that and say it is not my responsibility. I have to let him know that these things are out there, and he appreciates it. So again, that is another way we stay up on cyber technology. We wait for intelligence, and then we act on it.

Mr. GROSSI. We at the NFL, in the NFL IT department, we have a director position who is responsible for cybersecurity throughout the NFL. As with the Indy 500, we have a cross-communication plan. When you purchase your Super Bowl ticket, you can log in and receive and send text messages that we blast out information that is relevant to the game, relevant to events around the game, and we can receive information from these 70,000 or 80,000-plus fans that are in the city when they see something.

The physical security of the cyber part of Super Bowl is really done by the stadium where we are playing the game, and we lean heavily on the FBI and the Department of Homeland Security.

They come in and assess our cyber capabilities and our vulnerabilities, and we try to make the adjustments from there.

Mrs. BROOKS. Thank you.

Very briefly, Dr. Roberts, any comments you might have about what you have seen with stadiums you have worked with in cyber?

Mr. ROBERTS. Well, first of all, we have seen, at least in the last few years, a significant change in just the awareness that cyber is a serious issue. A few years ago when I interviewed some folks at a major NBA arena, they didn't even know that there were apps out there for the patrons, and they never connected the way to use the security folks connected with the fan folks. So that has changed.

The one thing I think I would mention is that the key to a lot of this is education. We have been just doing a project for DHS S&T on cybersecurity education and training, and certainly I think it is fair to say that 80 to 90 percent of cyber attacks could be prevented if everybody were just educated on what not to open and what attachments not to look at, and so on and so forth. There are some basic principles.

I think we have already seen it, both in the sports industry and many agencies around the country, that there is an increasing interest in education and training. That comes down ultimately to a long-term plan for how to educate and train folks in cyber. I know there are estimates that we may be short 700,000 cybersecurity experts within 5 years. So it is not just a stadium problem, but it certainly is one.

Mrs. BROOKS. Thank you.

I will now turn to Congressman Payne for another 5 minutes of questioning.

Mr. PAYNE. Thank you, Madam Chairwoman.

Dr. Roberts, you know that the CCICADA Center works on models of crowd management and on prevention of human trafficking at major sports events such as the Super Bowl. Can you talk about how CCICADA has worked with MetLife Stadium to improve security for mass gatherings such as the Super Bowl? How has your work been integrated into security plans?

Mr. ROBERTS. So, we have been welcomed at MetLife. Mr. DeLorenzi has given us, first of all, access to his own personal expertise. We have been allowed to follow him around on game days and preparation for game days. We have been given access to the command center. We have been given access to the stadium to observe the screening procedures, and we have been in on some of the discussions about how to change things.

So just by way of an example, with the implementation of the magnetometers, we did a little bit of modeling to help MetLife decide how many they might need and what kind of physical changes might be necessary, and then most recently there was the first experiment with the new magnetometer system just this month at a soccer game between Portugal and Ireland.

I guess I shouldn't mention Portugal today.

[Laughter.]

Mr. ROBERTS. We were there at MetLife discussing how many you might need—it was not the full crowd; it was around 50,000—how you might arrange the tables and the screeners and who would stand where, and whose role would be what, and then we were there on game day. We took notes. We gathered a lot of data as to how long each of the lines would take. We compared it to the other gates which did the normal screening, and we are still processing that data. We shared some of it. We will share some of the rest of it, and I am sure that will lead to changes again. In fact, it already has led to some ideas as to how to involve randomization procedures.

Mr. PAYNE. Thank you.

Mr. ROBERTS. So working closely with the stadium has really been—it is a win for us, and I believe the stadium has also appreciated what we have done.

Mr. PAYNE. Excellent.

Mr. BOLES. As far as the modeling, the computer simulation, I will tell you how we use it, how we have used it to learn how to evacuate the stadium. Evacuating the stadium is the common denominator across any emergency, right? It is one of the things I worry about the most. I guess similar to 9/11 is getting people out of the building, and we are talking about 80,000 people. So I impress upon my staff that that is their role. We have a certain amount of police officers, amount of firemen, EMS, and they are going to be busy dealing with whatever emergency has created the evacuation scenario, and it is going to be left to us to get the people out of the building.

Prior to getting this modeling tool of evacuation, it is interesting, everybody in this room would probably have a different thought in their head as to what that might look like and how it might go, and how long it might take. Because we live in a time now where we can do simulations, computer simulations, we sat down with the Rutgers folks, DHS S&T and this company Regal, and we developed a model, and the model is all 80,000 people in their seats and how long it would take and what it would look like for these people to leave all at once, and we use it as a training tool for our civilian personnel. They sit there and they look at it and say, listen, it is no longer your imagination, this is what it is going to look like and this is how long it is going to take, and you need to make sure it happens.

They understand that, and it helps a lot. It also gave us—I won't discuss the times, but it tells us exactly how long it will take. It tells us how to do it, and not only for evacuation. Dr. Roberts said this earlier. It taught us how to bring people inside out of a severe lightning situation and where to put people and how to move people, and again, all done—we see this all the time on CNN. You can really simulate any situation on a computer now. It was some technology that was very, very useful. We are lucky to have it.

Mr. PAYNE. Madam Chairwoman, in the interest of time, I will yield back.

Mrs. BROOKS. Thank you.

I think this might be a good question to wrap up with because we have heard just amazing things that you all are doing in leading your organizations, and obviously the studies being done by Rutgers and Purdue and others. But I worry—and we heard this at our hearing last week in Washington, DC—how we could do a better job sharing these best practices, the wonderful things you are doing, whether or not the NFL shares with the NBA and with the different tracks around the country.

I am curious from each of you what type of platform or what type of idea might you have as to how we could as a country do a better job sharing your best practices or your lessons learned. I am sure that each of you, and as Mr. Boles has shared and as I know each of you has shared after each event, your after-action and all your ideas continue for the next event. But how can we take lessons from New Jersey and share them with Kansas City or with San Diego or with Chicago and Indianapolis?

Any thoughts and ideas you might have? Because that could be the Federal Government's role, whether it is DHS' role in protecting the homeland. I am just curious about any thoughts you might have. If anyone wants to take a stab at it, I would sure love to hear it.

Mr. Grossi, did you want to jump in? It looked like you were ready.

Mr. GROSSI. Sure. At the NFL, we do share our best practices, and we share them with the other sports leagues, and the information that we——

Mrs. BROOKS. I'm sorry. How is that done? What is the mechanism that you share?

Mr. GROSSI. The mechanism is shared through the stadiums, through the security department, the NFL security department, through baseball, through the NBA, and through the National Hockey League. There are different organizations, domestic security organizations where information is shared. I think the standard that the SAFETY Act certification, the level that has brought the stadiums to there, I think that would be a good responsibility of DHS. I think DHS can take the best of all the sports' best practices, disseminate them down. I will give you an example.

Baseball in 2015, I think they are all going to walk through magnetometers for all major league baseball games. We at the NFL have had metal detector screening for the last 2 years, and we are working towards that as well.

But I think the sharing of information from sports league to sports league is very good, and I think the Government could help that.

Mrs. BROOKS. Thank you.

Mr. DeLorenzi.

Mr. DELORENZI. There is another university, the University of Southern Mississippi, and they have actually established a formal committee that meets quarterly. We meet in different—the last time it was major league baseball, we met in the hockey office, and U.S. Tennis is there. We all get together in a room, and we will spend a day just talking about things we are talking about now. The last time we talked about credentialing and background checks.

So there is a formal committee right now that exists, and they should be recognized. That is Lou Marciani and, again, the University of Southern Mississippi who have gone out there and taken the lead, I think, in bringing everybody together, and he is doing a good job. We do get together in meetings, and I will look at the director of the NHL, and I will look at the director of NFL security, and the NBA, and tennis, and we will share and exchange ideas face to face.

Mrs. BROOKS. Thank you.

Mr. Boles.

Mr. BOLES. With respect to sharing ideas and maybe taking it a step further with something Dr. Roberts said, the Indianapolis Motor Speedway, unlike MetLife Stadium or a lot of these arenas and racetracks in general, we host three or four big events for the entire year. So we don't have 200-plus events where it makes a lot of sense to invest a lot of capital in different pieces of infrastructure.

However, there might be an opportunity as we bring a group together to look at organizations like the Indianapolis Motor Speedway, other race tracks, other smaller venues that may not have 200 events a year, and begin to do some equipment sharing. The magnetometer might be a great place for us to begin to look at are there ways that we can share those, and then spread that cost across several venues, and in addition maybe you take the staff that is trained and use them, and they can be mobile and run different facilities.

So that might be an opportunity we start thinking through, how do we share that information, maybe on some of the foundations that are already set, but there may be something in taking that one step further and looking at ways that we can share equipment and make it easier and more accessible for especially venues like ours that don't run a lot of events a year, but maybe then even some smaller venues where fiscally it just doesn't make sense for them to make that kind of investment.

Mrs. BROOKS. Thank you.

Dr. Roberts, we look forward and are pleased that you are working with DHS' Science and Technology Directorate and coming up with some of these. But with respect to whether it is your manual that is coming out and others, what is the best platform to be sharing all of these best practices?

Mr. ROBERTS. So, I wouldn't say that there is one best way to do it. We take advantage of every opportunity to bring people together and to bring ideas together. I don't want to repeat some of the things I have said before, but let me mention a couple of other examples.

One would be some of the firms that run the security for more than one venue. So it is not unusual, for instance, that a company would manage or be responsible for the security and the training of the security folks at venues in more than one league—NBA, NFL, et cetera. So having those people involved is a key piece of what I think information sharing would be.

The second thing to mention is that a lot of these employees, including employees at the Super Bowl, are not well-paid people who are brought in. Sometimes we have seen them with special events only trained for a few minutes at the last minute. So getting that training somehow coordinated and having manuals and best practices and testing the training, so on and so forth, is an important thing to do.

The last thing I would mention is a more informal idea, and that is every one of our venues, at least in the major sports, have really serious professionals who are there and manage security for them. But even the most serious professionals don't always see everything. So one of the recommendations we have made is have somebody from another venue just come by and watch what you do, follow you around on game day, see what your procedures are and your protocols. That is a very good way of sharing information informally.

Mrs. BROOKS. Thank you. Thank you very much.

I do want to thank all of the witnesses for their invaluable testimony and actually our Members for the questions.

There may be additional questions as to the first panel, and this panel as well, and we will ask you to respond in writing if you receive any additional questions.

I would like to know if Congressman Payne would like to make any closing remarks before I close.

Mr. PAYNE. Thank you, Madam Chairwoman. Let me just say that I think this was two outstanding panels in terms of talking about best practices and moving forward in information sharing. At the committee we have done a lot of work around interoperability, so it is one of the key issues that we focus on at the committee.

I would be remiss if I didn't thank Brad Stephens from Homeland Security Committee for everything he has done to have this hearing be a success.

I am just glad, Madam Chairwoman, that you were able to come to Newark and see it for yourself and have a good time.

Note that here in the State of New Jersey we have people dedicated to working to make sure that the homeland is safe, mass gatherings are safe, and just continue to evolve in terms of making sure that, irrespective of where you are in this Nation, that our citizens can go about their lives in a safe manner.

I am just delighted that you were able to come here to Newark. We will have to keep you longer next time.

Mrs. BROOKS. Thank you. Yes, thank you. We do have to get back to Washington, DC later today for votes, but I do want to just thank all of you for attending and for the effort that you took. Obviously, beyond sporting events, all of our large venues, whether it is our arts and music centers, could also learn from I think the outstanding work that is done in the sports industry in this country, and I just want to thank you all for your collaboration, for continuing to put the United States of America on the global map as to the place that hosts the world's finest sporting events.

So I want to thank you. As Congressman Pascrell mentioned earlier—and it was wonderful that he could share with us—we do want to be a resource to you and working with the Department of Homeland Security and other Federal agencies. So we look forward to hearing from you in the future as to whether or not you might have future needs.

I just want to thank NJIT for hosting us today and for everyone who put out such a great effort for holding this important hearing. Thank you.

This hearing now stands adjourned.
[Applause.]
[Whereupon, at 12:25 p.m., the subcommittee was adjourned.]

○

www.ingramcontent.com/pod-product-compliance
Lightning Source LLC
Chambersburg PA
CBHW080546290526
45790CB00006B/2578